W9-ABX-826

STEAM

point

A guide to integrating Science, Technology, Engineering, the Arts and Math through Common Core

Susan M. Riley

For information, address:

EducationCloset
742 Charingworth Road
Westminster, MD 21158

susan@educationcloset.com

ISBN-13: 978-1481165730
ISBN-10: 1481165739

EducationCloset is a resource that is dedicated as a place where Arts Integration, Technology and Innovation Converge. There is a tremendous wealth of information, resources, multimedia, and an online community at the touch of a button. To visit, just go to: http://educationcloset.com

Also from EducationCloset

Shake the Sketch: An Arts Integration Workbook (2012)

A Vocal Advocate: An Arts Advocacy Workbook (2012)

Visit our online bookstore at: http://educationcloset.com/bookstore

Also available at Amazon.com

t a b l e

OF CONTENTS

INTRODUCTION

Counterpoint. A term for music that is interdependent, yet can be separated into independent, purposeful parts. It is a musical style that requires precision, reasoning, creativity and a lot of risk. The master of this style was Bach and his music seems to suggest that he took great pride and pleasure in writing music that was both a puzzle to be solved and an intricate art to be appreciated. Counterpoint is truly a style of music that incorporates math, poetry, ingenuity and logic all in one beautiful package.

As a music student in college, I dreaded going to my first Music Theory IV class. This class was dedicated solely to analyzing counterpoint music. I thought this would be dull and difficult and it wasn't how I wanted to spend my final semester of my junior year. Yet, when we began to look at the pieces, listen to them as a whole and then tear them apart, the magic of counterpoint was so incredible that I found myself drawn to my homework just so that I could try and figure out how a composer could make all of the independent pieces work so seamlessly together to create an entirely new sound. This had to be the original "network".

We, of course, are a networked nation. We are a network of skills and ideas, struggles and triumphs, redundancy and innovation. We are a beautiful, complicated, terrifying, inspiring snowflake of everything that ever was and the promise of what is to come crystalized into one moment in the history of time. Our time is fleeting and the bonds that connect us are thin but strong. WE are a network.

Yet, as a whole, education does not address this fact. Education, in the broad, generalized term views subjects and content as silos of information and students as the recipients of knowledge. What is taught in one classroom lives on its own and teachers are the operators of a well-oiled machine. Administrators become mere quality control personnel, in charge of making sure that each student passes inspection by meeting standards set for an arbitrary high-stakes testing event. Sound like something out of the early 20th century? Of course it is - because this is how school was originally formatted. It worked well then, as it prepared students for the economy to which they would soon enter. The problem is that this has not been the reality of our workforce needs for a long time, yet our schools have not changed.

We need to acknowledge and accept that the economy has shifted, the world has become smaller and more open, and the expectations for competing and succeeding in this global network are radically different than in previous generations. We have heard this all before, and yet our schools still do not reflect this change with any continuity or integrity. If we both acknowledge and accept our new global reality, then it is time to take the steps necessary to shift our educational systems, culture, and curriculum to address these needs. Our schools should be constantly evolving, molded by the needs of the society to which our students and our parents are citizens. They must mirror the global network to which we all belong and provide a safe and secure environment for our children to take risks, be creative, practice collaboration and build skills that are needed in a 21st century workforce. Schools must become integrated network hubs where information is curated, shared, explored, and molded into new ways of seeing and being so that our children each have equitable opportunities to grow and be challenged to succeed.

Integration is not a new idea. We have been studying the effect of integrated study for over 40 years and have miles of accumulated data that says it works. In recent decades, there has been a rise in the interest in STEM (Science, Technology, Engineering and Mathematics) and Arts Integration as ways to both engage our students and prepare them for the unique challenges in this rapidly changing world. And while there is plenty of research that showcases the merits of both of these integrated approaches, the majority of schools either do not use these ideas or only do so at the most minimal of levels. Why is this? There are plenty of reasons for why it is difficult to move the needle when it comes to implementing an integrated curriculum. First, many teachers are nervous that they do not have the skills themselves to adequately teach integrated topics. Second, there are limited frameworks available to assist teachers in discovering how to find the elegant and authentic connections across and between contents. Third, it is difficult to know how to assess integrated units or concepts because it is often difficult to do so in "traditional" or summative ways.

This book is focused on the last two areas of concern. It is broken into three main sections: Curriculum Mapping, Lesson Seeds, and Assessments. These three sections are meant to lead teachers and administrators through the process of building an integrated curriculum that supports networked study and understanding with integrity. It is meant to be a resource for those who struggling with the "how" of creating integrated curriculum and for those who need some fresh ideas on their approach to teaching and learning. When working through integrated lessons, many teachers need a practical guide as both an example and as a place to jumpstart their own creative ideas. This allows teachers to get back to the craft of teaching and providing those learning opportunities that our students so desperately crave.

This book does not delve deeply into the "why" of integration, as this has been discussed at great length over many years. However, to answer the first topic of concern outlined previously, teachers do not need to have all of the answers. That is not their job. Instead, their job should be asking interesting questions and curating the resources for students to use to find their own answers. So if you or your colleagues are nervous about implementing integrated lessons for fear that you do not have the skills needed in another area, you can place that burden down. Additionally, the approach of this book is through the process of STEAM: Science, Technology, Engineering, Arts and Mathematics. This is an approach to teaching which makes natural connections across multiple contents in order for students to engage in the necessary thinking and creative practices reflective of a 21st century society. The content here is standards-based and uses the lens of both STEM and Arts Integration to enhance and deepen meaning of content for students, to provide an access point for learners of varying abilities, and as a way to engage both teachers and learners. By making purposeful connections in and through STEM and the Arts, all skills, processes, and subjects are strengthened and students gain a richer learning experience. **It's the STEAM Point: each subject can stand alone, but when they are added together in a precise way, they make music together.**

It is important to understand that an integrated curriculum still allows for key skills to be taught within distinct classes (ie: science skills should still be taught in science and art skills should still be taught in the art class). Instead, an integrated curriculum acknowledges that students have learned these skills elsewhere and you are using their knowledge in and of these skills to teach a broader topic or concept. This book, therefore, provides the framework for developing these lessons to both utilize the skills being taught in all subjects and for assessing these concepts authentically in both areas.

Great care has been taken throughout this book to ensure alignment to both the Common Core Standards, the principles and best practices that have been identified through research, and to the integrity of the subjects themselves. Please note that as education evolves, so too does our work. Therefore, do not allow this book to become a stagnant resource on your desk. Instead, use the information and ideas presented here as a starting line and adapt them to fit your needs and that of our changing educational systems.

There is a favorite professional development activity that I like to use to wrap up the learning from our sessions. I bring a large ball of yarn and ask the participants to form a large circle around me. I hold the end of the string and toss the ball of yarn to someone in the circle. They must provide one personal takeaway from the session out loud to the group, then hold the string and toss the ball to another participant. As this keeps going, a web forms between all of us of the ideas and impacts from the day. But if one person lets go of their string, the whole web falls apart. Indeed, we are a network and each of us have a key connection to understand, develop and pass along. Because we are only as strong as the ideas we share and the webs we weave.

Part 1: Curriculum Mapping

part
ONE

Building the Frame

Curriculum mapping is a critical component to building an integrated framework for lesson planning and finding natural connections across content areas. A curriculum map is simply a way to identify the standards you are trying to teach and the standards from other content areas that are similar or provide a natural match in teaching a skill or concept. Sometimes, the standards look very similar and in some cases even use the same language. Obviously, this is a natural match. However, there are also times when the standards may say different things but can complement each other in teaching a broader essential question or idea. Therefore, when creating curriculum maps, it is important to do so as an integrated team rather than as an isolated unit.

An excellent set of curriculum maps can save a lot of time and energy when creating integrated units or lessons of study. Often, teachers say that their biggest struggle with integration is the time that it takes; specifically the time that it takes to plan a lesson. Trying to find the standards that match can be time-consuming and frustrating. By creating a set of master curriculum maps that teachers can use and tweak to accommodate their individual curriculum guides, there is a great time savings and an assurance that the lessons have a strongly aligned standards spine.

The Curriculum Mapping Process

1. **Connected Conversations** A curriculum map is only as strong as the knowledge and ideas that are used to form it. If you are creating a curriculum map alone in a classroom somewhere and are not actively engaging in conversations with your colleagues in these

areas you are trying to align, your map with have holes in it that you cannot fill. Remember: you cannot possibly know everything. So, part of the richness of a curriculum map comes from these connected conversations about what standards you are trying to teach and how these might be aligned in some way. Of course, these connected conversations are a great way to find out if there is NOT a natural or authentic connection. This is perfectly fine, because as in life, not everything connects. You never want to force an alignment that is not there at its core. My favorite example of this is when 2nd grade teachers who are studying the 50 states try to claim that there is a natural alignment between their social studies standard and using the song "50 Nifty United States" to help students remember the state names. While this might be engaging for students and may even look like a natural connection, there is nothing natural about this connection. What music standard are you meeting by using that song in the social studies classroom in 2nd grade? The piece is a challenging rhythm, has a melodic range more suited for 5th grade and maintaining an accurate steady beat is difficult. How would a social studies teacher know that? This is why those connected conversations are critical to developing outstanding curriculum maps that maintain the integrity of both contents that are being aligned.

2. **Finding the Elegant Fit.** The next step after having those rich dialogues is to identify what exactly you want students to know and understand. These could be skills or it could be a broad topic or concept. Once you have this, you'll need to look at what standards this addresses in both content areas. This becomes your Elegant Fit: where the standards align. You'll right them down side-by-side so that you can keep the importance of both standards at the forefront of your mind.

3. **Assessment Choice.** After you have found the naturally-aligned standards and you know what you want your students to be able to know or do, you need to immediately decide how you would like to assess them. There are a variety of ways to do this, and there is a whole section of this book dedicated to this process. The key here is to understand that you must develop the assessment immediately following aligning your standards. This is imperative because you need to have the end in mind when developing your lesson plan to ensure that you are meeting the goals and standards you set forth at the beginning of the lesson itself. You need to hit your target and by writing

your assessment next, you set a clear expectation for yourself of what target you are placing in front of your students.

4. **Writing the lesson.** Now that you have the major components outlined and aligned, the easy part has arrived. You can now write the lesson, ensuring that you are constantly referencing and teaching both standards you placed at the top of your lesson and that you are providing a process to get students to be able to meet the target you set with your assessment choice.

5. **Reflection.** Once you have completed the lesson, you come back together with your original colleagues and have another connected conversation to discuss what went well, what may need tweaked, what you learned about your students and yourself as a teacher and what comes next. Then, you get to do the whole process over again!

Sometimes, the most challenging part of the Curriculum Mapping Process is in developing an idea you'd like to explore as an integrated lesson or unit. It can be difficult to narrow in on a topic and yet allow it to be hearty enough that many other areas can have an authentic connection. What follows is a graphic that you can use to help you with this part of the process. You can use this to work through the idea process. Then, once it's filled out, it's much easier to know what you'd like to map out and align.

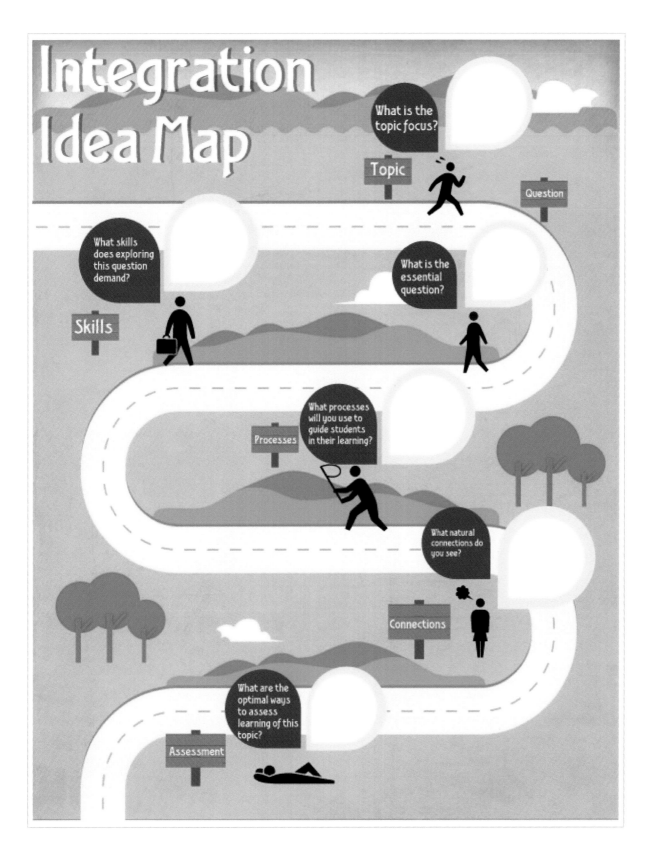

Curriculum Mapping Core-Aligned Samples

Now that you understand the curriculum mapping process, the rest of this section will be dedicated to providing you with Common Core-Aligned Integrated Curriculum Map Samples, Resources and Templates to help move you forward in this part of the design process. You will see a variety of ways that you can interpret Curriculum Mapping through these samples, as well as many great ideas for Common Core Integrated Lesson Seeds. And while many of these have been done as a way to begin to build your curriculum map libraries, this is certainly not an exhaustive list - merely a set to get you started.

Common Core English Language Arts Integrated Curriculum Maps

These maps have been aligned to the Anchor Standards in Common Core English Language Arts. These anchor standards span from grades K-12 in the areas of Reading, Writing, Speaking and Listening and Language. These anchor standards were chosen for their broad range, yet specific focus in each area. Keep in mind, however, that it may be a good idea to align the anchor standard and indicator you would like to meet as a way to narrow your integration focus even further.

The format of these maps provides clarity and some idea kickstarters. This curriculum map grouped the anchor standards together and then broke out each standard individually. Additionally, the fine arts standards are being revised as of this writing and it was not practical to reference individual state curriculum indicators for each broad standard. Therefore, the standards used for the fine arts are based on the current 2012 national standards for Visual Art, Music, Dance and Theatre. Finally, there are currently no national STEM standards or practices. The practices referenced in the following charts are based on the Maryland STEM Standards of Practice. These can be found in Appendix C.

Common Core Standard - this column provides the specific ELA standard of focus

Naturally-Aligned Fine Arts Standards - this column provides a naturally aligned standard in Visual Art, Music, Dance and/or Theatre based on the broad national standards for each subject. Again, in your curriculum maps, it may be a good idea to look at your state's approved curriculum for the fine arts areas and located specific indicators that fall within these broad standards to narrow your focus.

Naturally-Aligned STEM Practices - these are STEM Standards of Practice from Maryland that provide a natural link to the Common Core ELA Standard, either in the standard itself or in the possible implementation of that standard. You may also find the indicators for the practices by going to the STEM Standards of Practice resource located in Appendix C.

Lesson Idea Thread - This is a lesson seed idea that integrates one or more of the fine arts standards, and/or STEM practices to align with the matching ELA Standard. These Lesson Ideas can be used to build a lesson plan or start a connected conversation. Additionally, there are lesson idea threads provided for grades K-12 in these samples.

Common Core Integrated Curriculum Map - English Language Arts

	Common Core ELA Standards	Naturally-Aligned Fine Arts Standards	Naturally-Aligned STEM Practices	Lesson Idea Thread
Anchor Standards: Reading	CCSS.ELA-Literacy.CCRA.R.1 Read closely to determine what the text says explicitly and to make logical inferences from it; cite specific textual evidence when writing or speaking to support conclusions drawn from the text.	**Art**: 3. Choosing and evaluating a range of subject matter, symbols, and ideas. **Music**: 5. Reading and notating music. 6. Listening to, analyzing, and describing music. **Dance**: 4. Applying and demonstrating critical and creative thinking skills in dance. **Theatre**: 5. Researching by finding information to support classroom dramatizations.	3. Interpret and Communicate Information in Science, Technology, Engineering and Math. 5. Engage in Logical Reasoning	**Grades 3-5:** Read a selection of music notation from Tchaikovsky's Peter and the Wolf. Determine the mood of the piece based upon the textual evidence (tempo, instrumentation, rhythms, etc). Then, read an excerpt from the same section of the folk story. Compare and contrast the selections using evidence from each. **Standards**: R.1, Music 5, STEM 5
	CCSS.ELA-Literacy.CCRA.R.2 Determine central ideas or themes of a text and analyze their development; summarize the key supporting details and ideas.	**Art**: 3. Choosing and evaluating a range of subject matter, symbols, and ideas. **Music**: 6. Listening to, analyzing, and describing music. **Dance**: 4. Applying and demonstrating critical and creative thinking skills in dance.	3. Interpret and Communicate Information in Science, Technology, Engineering and Math. 4. Engage in Inquiry	**Grades K-2:** View a scene from The Nutcracker ballet and determine the main idea of that scene and what details support that idea. Have students describe how the choreography used in the ballet showcases the details that contribute to the whole scene. **Standards**: R.2, Dance 4, STEM 4
	CCSS.ELA-Literacy.CCRA.R.3 Analyze how and why individuals, events, or ideas develop and interact over the course of a text.	**Art**: 2. Using knowledge of structures and functions. **Music**: 6. Listening to, analyzing, and describing music. **Dance**: 2. Understanding the choreographic principles, processes, and structures. **Theatre**: 7. Analyzing and explaining personal preferences and constructing meanings from classroom dramatizations.	2. Integrate Science, Technology, Engineering and Math Content. 3. Interpret and Communicate Information in Science, Technology, Engineering and Math.	**Grades 7-9:** Read a scene from West Side Story and describe the relationships between the characters. Listen to the music and watch the choreography: how does the music and dance support the intricate balance between all of the characters? **Standards**: R.3, Theatre 7, Music 6, Dance 2.

Common Core Integrated Curriculum Map - English Language Arts

<table>
<tr><th></th><th>Common Core ELA Standards</th><th>Naturally-Aligned Fine Arts Standards</th><th>Naturally-Aligned STEM Practices</th><th>Lesson Idea Thread</th></tr>
<tr>
<td rowspan="2">Anchor Standards: Reading</td>
<td>CCSS.ELA-Literacy.CCRA.R.4 Interpret words and phrases as they are used in a text, including determining technical, connotative, and figurative meanings, and analyze how specific word choices shape meaning or tone.</td>
<td>Art: 2. Using knowledge of structures and functions. Music: 6. Listening to, analyzing, and describing music. Dance: 3. Understanding dance as a way to create and communicate meaning. Theatre: 2. Acting by assuming roles and interacting in improvisations.</td>
<td>2. Integrate Science, Technology, Engineering and Math Content. 3. Interpret and Communicate Information in Science, Technology, Engineering and Math.</td>
<td>Grades 9-12: View a piece of DiVinci's artwork. Read the art through its use of shading, proportions, and mathematical congruity. Determine how DiVinci's intentional use of these elements shaped the meaning of the piece. Standards: R.4, Art 2, STEM 2, 3</td>
</tr>
<tr>
<td>CCSS.ELA-Literacy.CCRA.R.5 Analyze the structure of texts, including how specific sentences, paragraphs, and larger portions of the text (e.g., a section, chapter, scene, or stanza) relate to each other and the whole.</td>
<td>Art: 2. Using knowledge of structures and functions. Music: 6. Listening to, analyzing, and describing music. 7. Evaluating music and music performances. Dance: 2. Understanding the choreographic principles, processes, and structures. Theatre: 2. Acting by assuming roles and interacting in improvisations. 4. Directing by planning classroom dramatizations.</td>
<td>2. Integrate Science, Technology, Engineering and Math Content.</td>
<td>Grades 4-6: Listen to a selection from Beethoven's Eroica Symphony and ask students to analyze how the phrasing that was used contributed to the overall meaning of the piece. Interpret how the mathematics of music notation was used in this meter to showcase a moment of history. Standards: R.5, Music 6, STEM 2</td>
</tr>
</table>

Education Closet

Common Core Integrated Curriculum Map - English Language Arts

	Common Core ELA Standards	Naturally-Aligned Fine Arts Standards	Naturally-Aligned STEM Practices	Lesson Idea Thread
Anchor Standards: Reading	CCSS.ELA-Literacy.CCRA.R.6 Assess how point of view or purpose shapes the content and style of a text.	**Art**: 4. Understanding the visual arts in relation to history and cultures. **Music**: Understanding music in relation to history and culture. **Dance**: 3. Understanding dance as a way to create and communicate meaning. 5. Demonstrating and understanding dance in various cultures and historical periods. **Theatre**: 1. Script writing by planning and recording improvisations based on personal experience and heritage, imagination, literature, and history. 7. Analyzing and explaining personal preferences and constructing meanings from classroom dramatizations and from theatre, film, television, and electronic media productions.	4. Engage in Inquiry 5. Engage in Logical Reasoning	**Grades K-3:** Read a scene from Where the Wild Things Are. Have each student perform that scene as if they were Max. Analyze how this might change the message of the story. **Standards**: R.6, Theatre 1, STEM 4, 5
	CCSS.ELA-Literacy.CCRA.R.7 Integrate and evaluate content presented in diverse media and formats, including visually and quantitatively, as well as in words.	**Art**: 3. Choosing and evaluating a range of subject matter, symbols, and ideas. **Music**: 8. Understanding relationships between music, the other arts, and disciplines outside the arts. **Dance**: 6. Making connections between dance and other disciplines. **Theatre**: 6. Comparing and connecting art forms by describing theatre, dramatic media (such as film, television, and electronic media), and other art forms.	2. Integrate Science, Technology, Engineering and Math Content. 3. Interpret and Communicate Information in Science, Technology, Engineering and Math.	**Grades 6-9:** Investigate the evolving connections between dance and technology (such as iLuminate) and using both to communicate content to various audiences. Suggested article: http://bit.ly/S5kMtQ **Standards**: R.7, Dance 6, STEM 3
	CCSS.ELA-Literacy.CCRA.R.8 Delineate and evaluate the argument and specific claims in a text, including the validity of the reasoning as well as the relevance and sufficiency of the evidence.	**Art**: 5. Reflecting upon and assessing the characteristics and merits of their work and the work of others. **Music**: 7. Evaluating music and music performances.	3. Interpret and Communicate Information in Science, Technology, Engineering and Math. 5. Engage in Logical Reasoning.	**Grades 9-12:** Review the song "Ohio" by Crosby, Stills, Nash and Young. Have students complete a text analysis of the lyrics and research the event at Kent State to determine if the claims made by the lyrics were accurate and substantiated by evidence. How did the song convey this differently than news outlets at the time? **Standards**: R.8, Music 7

Common Core Integrated Curriculum Map - English Language Arts

	Common Core ELA Standards	Naturally-Aligned Fine Arts Standards	Naturally-Aligned STEM Practices	Lesson Idea Thread
Anchor Standards: Reading	CCSS.ELA-Literacy.CCRA.R.9 Analyze how two or more texts address similar themes or topics in order to build knowledge or to compare the approaches the authors take.	**Art**: 1. Understanding and applying media, techniques, and processes. **Music**: 6. Listening to, analyzing, and describing music. **Dance**: 2. Understanding the choreographic principles, processes, and structures. **Theatre**: 7. Analyzing and explaining personal preferences and constructing meanings from classroom dramatizations and from theatre, film, television, and electronic media productions.	2. Integrate Science, Technology, Engineering and Math Content. 3. Interpret and Communicate Information in Science, Technology, Engineering and Math. 6. Collaborate as a STEM team.	**Grades 3-5:** View pieces by Matisse and Picasso. Determine how these two artists communicated similar topics through their work and what set each of them apart. **Standards:** R.9, Art 1
	CCSS.ELA-Literacy.CCRA.R.10 Read and comprehend complex literary and informational texts independently and proficiently.	**Art**: 1. Understanding and applying media, techniques, and processes. **Music**: 5. Reading and notating music. **Dance**: 1. Identifying and demonstrating movement elements and skills in performing dance. **Theatre**: 2. Acting by assuming roles and interacting in improvisations.	3. Interpret and Communicate Information in Science, Technology, Engineering and Math.	**Grades 7-10:** Read portions of Homer's Odyssey and act out the scenes through individual interpretations. Discuss the context within the engineering and technology at the time. **Standards**: R.10, Theatre 2, STEM 3
Anchor Standards: Writing	CCSS.ELA-Literacy.CCRA.W.1 Write arguments to support claims in an analysis of substantive topics or texts using valid reasoning and relevant and sufficient evidence.	**Art**: 5. Reflecting upon and assessing the characteristics and merits of their work and the work of others. **Music**: 7. Evaluating music and music performances.	1. Learn and apply rigorous Science, Technology, Engineering and Math content. 3. Interpret and Communicate Information in Science, Technology, Engineering and Math. 5. Engage in Logical Reasoning.	**Grades 3-5:** View Starry Night by Van Gogh and assess the use of art elements (color, shape, line, texture) in communicating his point of view. Examine how these same elements are used in mathematics, architecture and design today. **Standards:** W.1, Art 5, STEM 1, 3

Common Core Integrated Curriculum Map - English Language Arts

<table>
<tr><th></th><th>Common Core ELA Standards</th><th>Naturally-Aligned Fine Arts Standards</th><th>Naturally-Aligned STEM Practices</th><th>Lesson Idea Thread</th></tr>
<tr>
<td rowspan="3">Anchor Standards: Writing</td>
<td>CCSS.ELA-Literacy.CCRA.W.2 Write informative/ explanatory texts to examine and convey complex ideas and information clearly and accurately through the effective selection, organization, and analysis of content.</td>
<td>Art: 5. Reflecting upon and assessing the characteristics and merits of their work and the work of others.
Music: 7. Evaluating music and music performances.
Theatre: 1. Script writing by planning and recording improvisations based on personal experience and heritage, imagination, literature, and history.</td>
<td>1. Learn and apply rigorous Science, Technology, Engineering and Math content.

3. Interpret and Communicate Information in Science, Technology, Engineering and Math.

5. Engage in Logical Reasoning.</td>
<td>Grades 5-8: Write a journalistic script on a current news topic and perform the scene for their peers. Students should be sure to include pertinent details of the situation through interviews, voice overs and/or debates. Students will need to research the topic at length prior to writing their script.
Standards: W.2, Theatre 1, STEM 1,3</td>
</tr>
<tr>
<td>CCSS.ELA-Literacy.CCRA.W.3 Write narratives to develop real or imagined experiences or events using effective technique, well-chosen details and well-structured event sequences.</td>
<td>Art: 1. Understanding and applying media, techniques, and processes.
Music: 4. Composing and arranging music within specified guidelines.
Dance: 2. Understanding the choreographic principles, processes, and structures.
Theatre: 1. Script writing by planning and recording improvisations based on personal experience and heritage, imagination, literature, and history.</td>
<td>1. Learn and apply rigorous Science, Technology, Engineering and Math content.

3. Interpret and Communicate Information in Science, Technology, Engineering and Math.

5. Engage in Logical Reasoning.</td>
<td>Grades K-2: Create a dance to tell a story of events. The dance should include various shapes and lines to communicate a story sequence that uses beginning, middle and end.
Standards: W.3, Dance 2, STEM 5</td>
</tr>
<tr>
<td>CCSS.ELA-Literacy.CCRA.W.4 Produce clear and coherent writing in which the development, organization, and style are appropriate to task, purpose, and audience.</td>
<td>Art: 1. Understanding and applying media, techniques, and processes.
Music: 4. Composing and arranging music within specified guidelines.
Dance: 2. Understanding the choreographic principles, processes, and structures.
Theatre: 1. Script writing by planning and recording improvisations based on personal experience and heritage, imagination, literature, and history.</td>
<td>3. Interpret and Communicate Information in Science, Technology, Engineering and Math.</td>
<td>Grades 3-6: Compose a piece of music which communicates a clear idea on a current world event. The piece should be notated and performed using music software if possible (ie: Garageband, Aurelius, etc).
Standards: W.4, Music 4, STEM 3</td>
</tr>
</table>

Common Core Integrated Curriculum Map - English Language Arts

	Common Core ELA Standards	Naturally-Aligned Fine Arts Standards	Naturally-Aligned STEM Practices	Lesson Idea Thread
Anchor Standards: Writing	CCSS.ELA-Literacy.CCRA.W.5 Develop and strengthen writing as needed by planning, revising, editing, rewriting, or trying a new approach.	**Art**: 2. Using knowledge of structures and functions. 5. Reflecting upon and assessing the characteristics and merits of their work and the work of others. **Music**: 3. Improvising melodies, variations, and accompaniments. 4. Composing and arranging music within specified guidelines. **Dance**: 2. Understanding the choreographic principles, processes, and structures. **Theatre**: 1. Script writing by planning and recording improvisations based on personal experience and heritage, imagination, literature, and history. 3. Designing by visualizing and arranging environments for classroom dramatizations. 4. Directing by planning classroom dramatizations.	6. Collaborate as a STEM Team.	**Grades 2-4:** Create a short scene advertising a new product. Direct 2 or 3 versions of the scene and then test-market it with another class to gain feedback and edit as necessary. **Standards**: W.5, Theatre 1, STEM 6
	CCSS.ELA-Literacy.CCRA.W.6 Use technology, including the Internet, to produce and publish writing and to interact and collaborate with others.	**Theatre**: 8. Understanding context by recognizing the role of theatre, film, television, and electronic media in daily life.	6. Collaborate as a STEM Team. 7. Apply Technology Strategically.	**Grades 1-3:** Write and publish a story based on illustrations through Storybird.com or LittleBirdTales.com **Standards**: W.6, STEM 7
	CCSS.ELA-Literacy.CCRA.W.7 Conduct short as well as more sustained research projects based on focused questions, demonstrating understanding of the subject under investigation.	**Art**: 4. Understanding the visual arts in relation to history and cultures. **Music**: Understanding music in relation to history and culture. **Dance**: 5. Demonstrating and understanding dance in various cultures and historical periods. **Theatre**: 5. Researching by finding information to support classroom dramatizations.	1. Learn and apply rigorous Science, Technology, Engineering and Math content. 3. Interpret and Communicate Information in Science, Technology, Engineering and Math. 4. Engage in Inquiry.	**Grades 6-8**: Research Steve Jobs and Bill Gates under the topic "Understanding and Marketing the Elements of Design". Write a report on the history of how these two men changed how we use technology through incorporating the elements of design. **Standards**: W.7, Art 4, STEM 3,4

Common Core Integrated Curriculum Map - English Language Arts

	Common Core ELA Standards	Naturally-Aligned Fine Arts Standards	Naturally-Aligned STEM Practices	Lesson Idea Thread
Anchor Standards: Writing	CCSS.ELA-Literacy.CCRA.W.8 Gather relevant information from multiple print and digital sources, assess the credibility and accuracy of each source, and integrate the information while avoiding plagiarism.	**Art**: 2. Using knowledge of structures and functions. **Music**: 6. Listening to, analyzing and describing music. **Dance**: 4. Applying and demonstrating critical and creative thinking skills in dance. **Theatre**: 5. Researching by finding information to support classroom dramatizations.	2. Integrate Science, Technology, Engineering and Math Content. 3. Interpret and Communicate Information in Science, Technology, Engineering and Math. 7. Apply Technology Strategically.	**Grades 9-12**: Study a variety of artistic sketchbooks of Edgar Degas. Analyze his use of line, subject, shading, and light in his work. Incorporate this information into an original work and blog about it using an Artist's Statement. **Standards**: W.8, Art 2, STEM 7
	CCSS.ELA-Literacy.CCRA.W.9 Draw evidence from literary or informational texts to support analysis, reflection, and research.	**Art**: 6. Making connections between visual arts and other disciplines. **Music**: 8. Understanding relationships between music, the other arts, and disciplines outside the arts. **Dance**: 6. Making connections between dance and other disciplines. **Theatre**: 6. Comparing and connecting art forms by describing theatre, dramatic media (such as film, television, and electronic media), and other art forms.	2. Integrate Science, Technology, Engineering and Math Content. 3. Interpret and Communicate Information in Science, Technology, Engineering and Math. 7. Apply Technology Strategically.	**Grades 6-8**: Conduct research on Mozart's musical interpretations and works through his letters to his family. Write a report describing how he wove his personal interpretations of music through the accepted musical traditions of the time. **Standards**: W.9, Music 8
	CCSS.ELA-Literacy.CCRA.W.10 Write routinely over extended time frames (time for research, reflection, and revision) and shorter time frames (a single sitting or a day or two) for a range of tasks, purposes, and audiences.	**Art**: 1. Understanding and applying media, techniques, and processes. **Music**: 4. Composing and arranging music within specified guidelines. **Dance**: 1. Identifying and demonstrating movement elements and skills in performing dance. **Theatre**: 1. Script writing by planning and recording improvisations based on personal experience and heritage, imagination, literature, and history.	3. Interpret and Communicate Information in Science, Technology, Engineering and Math.	**Grades K-3**: Practice writing in Artful Journals across subject areas throughout the day. Make notations, write reflections, draw sketches, and create collages to connect big ideas across content areas. Share these with teachers in each subject periodically. **Standards**: W.10, Art 1, STEM 3

Education Closet

Common Core Integrated Curriculum Map - English Language Arts

	Common Core ELA Standards	Naturally-Aligned Fine Arts Standards	Naturally-Aligned STEM Practices	Lesson Idea Thread
Anchor Standards: Speaking and Listening	CCSS.ELA-Literacy.CCRA.SL.1 Prepare for and participate effectively in a range of conversations and collaborations with diverse partners, building on others' ideas and expressing their own clearly and persuasively.	**Art**: 6. Making connections between visual arts and other disciplines. **Music**: 8. Understanding relationships between music, the other arts, and disciplines outside the arts. **Dance**: Making connections between dance and other disciplines. **Theatre**: 6. Comparing and connecting art forms by describing theatre, dramatic media (such as film, television, and electronic media), and other art forms.	3. Interpret and Communicate Information in Science, Technology, Engineering and Math. 6. Collaborate as a STEM team.	**Grades 4-6**: Create teams of students into "architectural firms" who must each create a design for a new shopping center. The design must be aesthetically pleasing, incorporate "Green" elements, and be cost effective. They must work together using Google SketchUp to create their design and present it to the shopping committee. A 3-D Model can be created based on the Google SketchUp drawing. **Standards**: SL.1, Art 6, STEM 3,6
	CCSS.ELA-Literacy.CCRA.SL.2 Integrate and evaluate information presented in diverse media and formats, including visually, quantitatively, and orally.	**Art**: 3. Choosing and evaluating a range of subject matter, symbols, and ideas. **Music**: 8. Understanding relationships between music, the other arts, and disciplines outside the arts. **Dance**: Making connections between dance and other disciplines. **Theatre**: 6. Comparing and connecting art forms by describing theatre, dramatic media (such as film, television, and electronic media), and other art forms.	3. Interpret and Communicate Information in Science, Technology, Engineering and Math. 7. Apply Technology Strategically.	**Grades 9-12**: Develop an online portfolio that clearly demonstrates their understanding of a specific topic of research through written reflections, multimedia presentations, and design. **Standards**: SL.2, Art 3, STEM 3, 7
	CCSS.ELA-Literacy.CCRA.SL.3 Evaluate a speaker's point of view, reasoning, and use of evidence and rhetoric.	**Art**: 4. Understanding the visual arts in relation to history and cultures. **Music**: 9. Understanding music in relation to history and culture. **Dance**: 3. Understanding dance as a way to create and communicate meaning. 5. Demonstrating and understanding dance in various cultures and historical periods. **Theatre**: 2. Acting by assuming roles and interacting in improvisations. 7. Analyzing and explaining personal preferences and constructing meanings from classroom dramatizations and from theatre, film, television, and electronic media productions.	3. Interpret and Communicate Information in Science, Technology, Engineering and Math. 5. Engage in Logical Reasoning.	**Grades 6-8**: Each student should create a piece of artwork, music, dance or dramatic presentation that communicates their point of view on a singular topic. This work should be a statement and if being presented orally, should be no more than 2 minutes in length. Students will then provide instant feedback through a Twitter feed or TodaysMeet.com wall evaluating the presenter's point of view. **Standards:** SL.3, Art 4, Music 9, Dance 3,5, Theatre 2,7, STEM 3, 5

Common Core Integrated Curriculum Map - English Language Arts

	Common Core ELA Standards	Naturally-Aligned Fine Arts Standards	Naturally-Aligned STEM Practices	Lesson Idea Thread
Anchor Standards: Speaking and Listening	CCSS.ELA-Literacy.CCRA.SL.4 Present information, findings, and supporting evidence such that listeners can follow the line of reasoning and the organization, development, and style are appropriate to task, purpose, and audience.	**Art**: 1. Understanding and applying media, techniques, and processes. **Music**: 4. Composing and arranging music within specified guidelines. **Dance**: 2. Understanding the choreographic principles, processes, and structures. **Theatre**: 1. Script writing by planning and recording improvisations based on personal experience and heritage, imagination, literature, and history.	1. Learn and apply rigorous Science, Technology, Engineering and Math content. 3. Interpret and Communicate Information in Science, Technology, Engineering and Math. 5. Engage in Logical Reasoning.	**Grades 3-5**: Students will create a wax museum. Each student will choose a historical figure to study and will develop a paragraph that summarizes the life and significant contributions of that figure. They will then portray that figure when they are tapped by "museum-goers" and perform their researched paragraph in the 1st person. **Standards:** SL.4, Theatre 1, STEM 3
	CCSS.ELA-Literacy.CCRA.SL.5 Make strategic use of digital media and visual displays of data to express information and enhance understanding of presentations.	**Art**: 1. Understanding and applying media, techniques, and processes. **Theatre:** 3. Designing by visualizing and arranging environments for classroom dramatizations	7. Apply Technology Strategically.	**Grades 3-5**: Study the artistic technique of Stippling (using dots to create an image). Create a Stipple graph highlighting major points of data to communicate a larger idea. **Standards:** SL.5, Art 1
	CCSS.ELA-Literacy.CCRA.SL.6 Adapt speech to a variety of contexts and communicative tasks, demonstrating command of formal English when indicated or appropriate.	**Art**: 3. Choosing and evaluating a range of subject matter, symbols and ideas. **Music**: 1. Singing, alone and with others a variety of repertoire. 6. Listening to, analyzing and describing music. **Dance**: 3. Understanding dance as a way to create and communicate meaning. **Theatre**: 2. Acting by assuming roles and interacting in improvisations.	3. Interpret and Communicate Information in Science, Technology, Engineering and Math. 7. Apply Technology Strategically.	**Grades K-2:** Perform the story of The Little Red Hen with each student becoming a part of the story. Students should alter how they use their voices and bodies to communicate as their chosen character. **Standards:** SL.6, Theatre 2
Language	CCSS.ELA-Literacy.CCRA.L.1 Demonstrate command of the conventions of standard English grammar and usage when writing or speaking.	**Theatre**: 1. Script writing by planning and recording improvisations based on personal experience and heritage, imagination, literature, and history.	3. Interpret and Communicate Information in Science, Technology, Engineering and Math.	**Grades 6-8** Write and perform an original one-act play that communicates a narrative story about immigration in America. **Standards:** L.1, Theatre 1, STEM 3

Common Core Integrated Curriculum Map - English Language Arts

Anchor Standards: Language

Common Core ELA Standards	Naturally-Aligned Fine Arts Standards	Naturally-Aligned STEM Practices	Lesson Idea Thread
CCSS.ELA-Literacy.CCRA.L.2 Demonstrate command of the conventions of standard English capitalization, punctuation, and spelling when writing.	**Art**: 4. Understanding the visual arts in relation to history and cultures. **Music**: 6. Listening to, analyzing and describing music.	3. Interpret and Communicate Information in Science, Technology, Engineering and Math.	**Grades 9-12** Select a set of repertoire for an upcoming musical recital (up to 12 pieces). Write the Program Notes for each selection, including a brief history of the piece of composer and its context. **Standards:** L.2, Music 6
CCSS.ELA-Literacy.CCRA.L.3 Apply knowledge of language to understand how language functions in different contexts, to make effective choices for meaning or style, and to comprehend more fully when reading or listening.	**Art**: 1. Understanding and applying media, techniques, and processes. **Music**: 4. Composing and arranging music within specified guidelines. **Dance**: 2. Understanding the choreographic principles, processes, and structures. **Theatre**: 1. Script writing by planning and recording improvisations based on personal experience and heritage, imagination, literature, and history.	3. Interpret and Communicate Information in Science, Technology, Engineering and Math.	**Grades 3-5**: Compose a piece of homophonic music with a singular chosen theme (ie: the seasons). Have students perform their piece for the class and then ask their classmates what they thought the theme was about, based on how they used the elements of music. **Standards**: L.3, Music 4
CCSS.ELA-Literacy.CCRA.L.4 Determine or clarify the meaning of unknown and multiple-meaning words and phrases by using context clues, analyzing meaningful word parts, and consulting general and specialized reference materials, as appropriate.	**Art**: 3. Choosing and evaluating a range of subject matter, symbols, and ideas. **Music**: 6. Listening to, analyzing, and describing music. **Dance**: 4. Applying and demonstrating critical and creative thinking skills in dance.	3. Interpret and Communicate Information in Science, Technology, Engineering and Math. 4. Engage in Inquiry 5. Engage in Logical Reasoning	**Grades 7-9**: View various works of Dutch art. Ask students to research the underlying meanings of certain elements of Dutch art and to use their knowledge in synthesizing the overall meaning of a Dutch piece of their choosing. **Standards**: L.4, Art 3, STEM 4, 5

Common Core Integrated Curriculum Map - English Language Arts

Anchor Standards: Language

Common Core ELA Standards	Naturally-Aligned Fine Arts Standards	Naturally-Aligned STEM Practices	Lesson Idea Thread
CCSS.ELA-Literacy.CCRA.L.5 Demonstrate understanding of figurative language, word relationships, and nuances in word meanings.	**Art**: 3. Choosing and evaluating a range of subject matter, symbols, and ideas. **Music**: 6. Listening to, analyzing, and describing music. **Dance**: 4. Applying and demonstrating critical and creative thinking skills in dance. **Theatre**: 7. Analyzing and explaining personal preferences and constructing meanings from classroom dramatizations and from theatre, film, television, and electronic media productions.	3. Interpret and Communicate Information in Science, Technology, Engineering and Math.	**Grades 2-4**: Read and analyze several Shel Silverstein poems. Have students dissect the pieces and analyze how Shel Silverstein uses words differently within his works. Write a poem in the style of Shel Silverstein and then perform it using practiced vocal inflections. **Standards**: L.5, Theatre 7
CCSS.ELA-Literacy.CCRA.L.6 Acquire and use accurately a range of general academic and domain-specific words and phrases sufficient for reading, writing, speaking, and listening at the college and career readiness level; demonstrate independence in gathering vocabulary knowledge when encountering an unknown term important to comprehension or expression.	**Art**: 3. Choosing and evaluating a range of subject matter, symbols, and ideas. **Music**: 6. Listening to, analyzing, and describing music. **Dance**: 4. Applying and demonstrating critical and creative thinking skills in dance. **Theatre**: 8. Understanding context by recognizing the role of theatre, film, television, and electronic media in daily life.	3. Interpret and Communicate Information in Science, Technology, Engineering and Math. 4. Engage in Inquiry 5. Engage in Logical Reasoning 7. Apply Technology Strategically.	**Grades 9-12**: Re-Enact the Second Continental Congress and the debate on July 2nd, 1776 on whether or not to declare independence from England. Allow for students in the audience to ask appropriate questions of the characters, who will then need to answer based on their knowledge from the time period and context. **Standards**: L.6, Theatre 8, STEM 3, 4, 5

Common Core Math Practices Integrated Maps

These maps provide alignment ideas for the Common Core Standards for Mathematical Practices, the Artistic Habits of Mind and the STEM Standards of Practice. The Standards for Mathematical Practices span grades K-12 and provide a broad lens for how to think about and use math as students move through each identified skill set. Because these practices are so broad, it doesn't make practical sense to try and align them with a specific fine arts standard. Therefore, the Artistic Habits of Mind (Appendix C) are practices that have been identified which artists use within the process of observing, creating, understanding and evaluating the arts. These make some very nice parallels to the Mathematical and STEM practices.

Common Core Mathematical Practice - the identified mathematical practice

Naturally-Aligned Artistic Habits of Mind - the habit of mind that makes an elegant fit with the identified mathematical practice. Some of these may repeat.

Naturally-Aligned STEM Practices - these are STEM Standards of Practice from Maryland that provide a natural link to the Common Core Mathematical Standards of Practice, either in the standard itself or in the possible implementation of that standard. You may also find the indicators for the practices by going to the STEM Standards of Practice resource located in Appendix C.

Common Core Math Standards Integrated Maps

These maps are generated for grades K-5 to provide a different example of how to use curriculum maps for Common Core alignment. This identifies alignments between selected Common Core Math Standards, Fine Arts Standards, STEM Practices and Lesson Idea Threads from grade K-5 as a way to show the relationship between the standards and each grade level.

Common Core Mathematical Standard - the identified mathematical standard.

Naturally-Aligned Fine Arts Standard - this column provides a naturally aligned standard in Visual Art, Music, Dance and/or Theatre based on a set of state standards (Maryland's) for each subject. This is to provide you with an alternate viewpoint of writing alignment maps that use an indicator, rather than a broad standard.

Naturally-Aligned STEM Practices - these are STEM Standards of Practice from Maryland that provide a natural link to the Common Core Mathematical Standards, either in the standard itself or in the possible implementation of that standard. You may also find the indicators for the practices by going to the STEM Standards of Practice resource located in Appendix C.

Lesson Idea Thread - This is a lesson seed idea that integrates one or more of the fine arts standards, and/or STEM practices to align with the matching Math Standard. These Lesson Ideas can be used to build a lesson plan or start a connected conversation. Additionally, there are lesson idea threads provided for grades K-5 in these samples.

Common Core Integrated Curriculum Map - Mathematical Practices

Common Core Math Practices	Naturally-Aligned Artistic Habits of Mind	Naturally-Aligned STEM Practices
1. Make sense of problems and persevere in solving them.	2. **Engage and Persist.** Learning to develop focus and other ways of thinking helpful to working and persevering at art tasks.	3. Interpret and communicate STEM Information. 4. Engage in inquiry.
2. Reason abstractly and quantitatively.	7. **Stretch and Explore.** Learning to reach beyond one's supposed limitations; to embrace the opportunity to learn from mistakes and accidents.	5. Engage in logical reasoning.
3. Construct viable arguments and critique the reasoning of others.	6. **Reflect.** Learning to think and talk with others about one's work and the process of making it.	3. Interpret and communicate STEM information.
4. Model with mathematics.	4. **Express.** Learning to create works that convey and idea, feeling or personal meaning.	2. Integrate STEM content.
5. Use appropriate tools strategically.	1. **Develop craft.** Learning to use tools and materials.	7. Apply technology Appropriately.
6. Attend to precision.	5. **Observe.** Learning to attend to visual, audible and written contexts more closely than ordinary "looking" requires.	3. Interpret and communicate STEM information.
7. Look for and make use of structure.	5. **Observe.** Learning to attend to visual, audible and written contexts more closely than ordinary "looking" requires.	1. Learn and apply rigorous STEM content.
8. Look for and express regularity in repeated reasoning.	4. **Express.** Learning to create works that convey and idea, feeling or personal meaning.	5. Engage in logical reasoning.

Common Core Integrated Curriculum Map - Mathematical Standards

Common Core Math Standard	Naturally-Aligned Fine Arts Standard	Naturally-Aligned STEM Practices	Lesson Idea Thread
Kindergarten: CCSS Math.Content.K.MD.B.3: Classify objects into given categories; count the numbers of objects in each category and sort the categories by count.	Music Standard K.3.a: Sort classroom instruments by sound and playing technique.	3. Interpret and communicate STEM Information. 5. Engage in logical reasoning	Sort and classify instruments from Carnival of the Animals by Camille Saint-Saens. Count how many instruments Saint-Saens used in his overall work.
1st grade: CCSS.Math.Content.1.G.A.2: Compose 2-dimensional shapes or 3-dimensional shapes to create a composite shape, and compose new shapes from the composite shape.	Visual Art Standard 1.3.1.c: Create artworks that explore the uses of color, line, shape, texture form and selected principles of design, such as pattern and repetition, to express ideas, thoughts and feelings.	1. Learn and apply rigorous STEM content. 2. Integrate STEM content.	Create a piece of artwork in the style of Picasso's Cubist period using select shapes.
2nd grade: CCSS.Math.Content.2.OA.B.2: Fluently add and subtract within 20 using mental strategies.	Dance Standard 2.3.1.b: Improvise variations on given short movement sequences through manipulation of body, space, time and energy	3. Interpret and communicate STEM information. 6. Collaborate as a STEM team.	Create and perform choreography within a beat pattern to demonstrate the ability to move within a certain measure of time, and to add or subtract movements to fit within a beat pattern.
3rd grade: CCSS.Math.Content.3.NF.A.3b: Recognize and generate simple equivalent fractions.	Music Standard 3.1.4.b: Write simple rhythm patterns from dictation using quarter notes, two connected eighth notes, half notes and corresponding rests.	1. Learn and apply rigorous STEM content. 2. Integrate STEM content.	Identify, use and play quarter, eighth, sixteenth, half and whole notes and record them using web-based applications to upload to iTunes.
4th grade: CCSS.Math.Content.4.NF.A.1: Explain why a fraction a/b is equivalent to a faction (nxa)(nxb) by using visual fraction models, with attention to how the number and size of the parts differ even though the two fractions themselves are the same size.	Visual Art Standard 4.3.1.a: Experiment with media, processes, and techniques to express thoughts and feelings that have personal meaning.	3. Interpret and Communicate STEM information. 7. Apply technology appropriately.	Create custom colors using the principles of hue both using color-mixing techniques with paint and online color-mixing technology.

Common Core Math Standard	Naturally-Aligned Fine Arts Standard	Naturally-Aligned STEM Practices	Lesson Idea Thread
5th grade: CCSS.Math.Content. 5.MD.B.2: Make a line plot to display a data set of measurements in fractions of a unit. Use operations on fractions for this grade to solve problems involving information presented in line plots.	Visual Art Standard 5.1.3.b: Select and use principles of design to create compositions that clarify ideas and feelings for the viewer.	2. Integrate STEM content 3. Interpret and communicate STEM information. 7. Apply technology appropriately.	Design an advertisement based on the latest performance data for a product.

Common Core Integrated Curriculum Map - Template

Common Core Standard	Naturally-Aligned Fine Arts Standard	Naturally-Aligned STEM Practice	Lesson Idea Thread

Curriculum maps provide a fantastic framework from which to build authentically designed and implemented integrated lesson plans. There are so many ways to approach curriculum mapping and the examples provided here just scratch the surface of what is out there. How you design your curriculum mapping is based upon the type of integration model you are pursuing. For example, you may find it easier to find an essential question that can be answered by many subject areas and to use those essential questions as the basis for your maps. There is no right or wrong way to approach curriculum mapping - the key is to maintain consistency in its implementation, to have a deep understanding of how your school or program is approach integration and to align your maps with that integration vision. Then, you can begin to design truly rich lessons and maintain the integrity of the integrated lesson that you seek.

Part 2: Lesson Seeds

part
TWO

Introduction

In this section, you will find 10 Integrated Lesson Seeds. Many of these are for Arts Integration, but there are plenty of opportunities for adaption to fit many topics. Each of these seeds identifies the Common Core State Standards being addresses, as well as the integrated content standards. Please note that at the time of this printing, the new national arts standards have not yet been released. Therefore, the standards being used for the Arts Integration lesson seeds are based upon the current standards that have been in place since 1994, and the adaptation being referenced is from the Maryland Fine Arts Standards, found here: http://mdk12.org/instruction/curriculum/arts/index.html. This is why the arts standards have been written out, so that when the new standards are released, you can match the current standard with the newest version.

Also, please note that these are lesson seeds for grades K-9. They are not lesson plans, nor should they be used as such. These provide an outline for a fully integrated lesson, but should be adjusted and extended as needed within each individual classroom. You are welcome to modify these lesson seeds at any time to fit your needs. And don't forget - there are new lesson seeds being posted all the time over at http://educationcloset.com/category/lesson-plans

Each lesson seed is also introduced through a short explanation, and is accompanied by any additional materials that have been outlined, as well as the standards that are being correlated. Please use these seeds as a way to jump start your integration efforts and as a general guideline for lesson writing.

Introduction

This is a great way to introduce opera to kids! Students begin with a composer study of Mozart, learn about opera, read the storyline of the libretto (story of the opera), and even develop their own opera scenes. This all requires skills in reading comprehension, plot development, fluency and activates prior knowledge. Plus, students are studying a classical composer, musical genre, form and melodic patterns. You really can't get more arts integration than this.

Grade Level: 2-3

Standards

Common Core	Fine Arts
R.I.2.1: Ask and answer such questions as *who, what, where, when, why*, and *how* to demonstrate understanding of key details in a text.	Music: Perform an ostinato while other students perform a contrasting ostinato. Music: Experience performance through singing, playing instruments, and listening to performances of others
R.I.2.6: Identify the main purpose of a text, including what the author wants to answer, explain, or describe.	

Education Closet

lesson seeds

THE MAGIC opera

READING AND MUSIC

Objectives

CONTENT	FINE ARTS
Reading: Students can read a story for comprehension and plot. CCSS.ELA-Literacy.RI.2.1, 2.6	**Music**: Students can perform melodic patterns (do-re-me). Students can demonstrate knowledge of a classical composer.

Materials:

* *The Magic Flute book*

* *The Magic Flute Opera DVD*

* Mozart's Musical Fantasy CD

* CD/DVD player

* Computer, LCD projector and internet

Extensions:

Create a Class Opera for an End-of-the-Year Culminating Activity!

1.) Engage students by acting as though you are the great composer, Wolfgang Amadeus Mozart. Tell them that you have come to visit to tell them about your amazing life. Provide them with the important details of Mozart's life and music through this activity (much can be found online about this).

2.) Have students explore Mozart's music and opera online through the website of the Metropolitan Opera (Met for Kids). Students can watch videos and gain an understanding of what opera is and how it is used to tell elaborate stories.

3.) Read "The Magic Flute" by Kyra Teis. Have students look at the illustrations and create still pictures of the scene with their bodies in groups (this is called Tableau). You can have them create scenes about what they think is happening and then read the pages, or you can have them create scenes for how the characters might feel based on what you've read.

4.) Listen to the "Mozart's Magical Fantasy", which tells a similar story based on the opera with the music of the opera in english. Have the students compare the two stories.

5.) Watch portions "The Magic Flute" opera on DVD to see how it can be brought to life. Create a web to illustrate how the story changes between the book, the CD and the opera itself.

6.) Listen to the Papageno/Papagena duet and have students form two lines. See if they can identify the d-r-m patterns. Then, have the girls sing the first pattern and the boys echo back. Listen to make sure that students are accurately singing on pitch and in rhythm.

Assessment:

<u>Students create their own "opera scene"!</u>
Have students re-create the Papageno/Papageno scene, but add their own interpretation. Write the scene, decide on costumes, add some instruments and dramatize their scene with the d-r-m patterned duet. **Look fors:** plot development and pattern accuracy.

Introduction

Within this lesson seed, our focus is on using dance to help guide vocabulary acquisition and an understanding of adjectives and verbs. Within the dance itself, the focus is on the elements of weight, space and time and accurately depicting the words chosen to describe a piece of music. This is written for Grade 3 Common Core ELA standards and integrated with Grade 3 dance standards.

Grade Level: 3-4

Standards

Common Core	Fine Arts
CCSS.ELA-Literacy.L.3.5b: Identify real-life connections between words and their use (e.g., describe people who are *friendly* or *helpful*).	Dance: Demonstrate knowledge of how elements of dance are used to communicate meaning
CCSS.ELA-Literacy.L.3.3a: Choose words and phrases for effect.	
CCSS.ELA-Literacy.L.3.1a: Explain the function of nouns, pronouns, verbs, adjectives, and adverbs in general and their functions in particular sentences.	

lesson seeds
WEIGHT IN words

VOCABULARY AND DANCE

Objectives

CONTENT	FINE ARTS
Common Core Reading: CCSS.ELA-Literacy.L.3.5b, CCSS.ELA-Literacy.L.3.3a, CCSS.ELA-Literacy.L.3.1a	Dance: Demonstrate knowledge of how elements of dance are used to communicate meaning

Materials:

•CD Player/iPod dock

•Board and writing tools (stylus, chalk, etc.)

•Samples of musical pieces.

•Chart paper

•Journals

•Pencils

•Room to move

1. Begin by playing a variety of musical examples with varying moods/textures. Some samples include: Flight of the Bumblebee, Beethoven's Pathetique Sonata, Mozart's Symphony No. 40, Elgar's Nimrod Symphony (IX).

2. Ask students to capture the essence of those pieces with one word. Probe for words that go beyond "sad", "happy", "excited". Be sure to have them search for the best word they can find in their memory banks that describe that piece.

3. Write the description words on the board in a list. Then, have the students move to their word for each piece.

4. In a separate column, ask students to describe one action word that would showcase their descriptive word in the other column. Again, avoid words like "jump" and look for more descriptive words like "leap".

5. Have students repeat step number 3, but this time, move as described by their action word.

6. Make one more column beside the other two. This time, have the students describe what kind of weight they would use in their body to demonstrate their action word (light and airy, loaded down by chains, etc).

7. Repeat step 5, but adding the weight of their action from their created list.

Assessment:

Writing in Color

Each student will write a brief journal entry that describes the essence of each song using their colorful vocabulary list generated in class. Each journal entry will also include a description of how they translated their labels into movement and how that made them feel.

Introduction

This lesson seed is so relevant for our times! We teach the most diverse classrooms America has ever seen. In this lesson, we look at immigration, the travel patterns of people, and what elements of culture are carried to each new place. Music is a perfect art source for integration and this lesson incorporates Poulenc's "Babar" to help describe how culture is always changing. This is great for the elementary grades, though it can be adjusted to be used in middle school by choosing a different story. This also allows for an opportunity to get to know more about your students – valuing where we all come from is essential in building a trusting and collaborative classroom for learning.

Grade Level: 3-4

Standards

Common Core	Fine Arts
CCSS.ELA-Literacy.RI.3.7 information gained from illustrations (e.g., maps, photographs) and the words in a text to demonstrate understanding of the text (e.g., where, when, why, and how key events occur).	Music: Students can describe how music influences culture.

lesson seeds

BABAR'S *travels*

S O C I A L   S T U D I E S   A N D   M U S I C

Objectives

CONTENT	FINE ARTS
Social Studies: Students can describe immigration paths. CCSS.ELA-Literacy.RI.3.7	**Music:** Students can describe how music influences culture.

Materials:

* "Babar" CD - Poulenc

* Shoebox designed as a treasure trunk

* papers, pencils

* The Story of Babar book.

* Various CD's of many music styles

Extensions:

Create a video from different areas of the world where students' families immigrated from and add music from those areas into the movie.

Lesson:

1.) Read the book "The Story of Babar" and discuss the various travels of Babar the elephant. Map these travels on the board or using a SmartBoard.

2.) Have a class discussion about where students' families came from. Students can gather information from home about where their families immigrated from.

3.) Listen to the piece "Babar" by Poulenc. Poulenc was affected in his travels by music from all areas of Europe. Have students describe how the music changes with each place Babar visits.

4.) After listening, place a large shoebox that has been decorated like a treasure box in the center of the room. Have students write down 2-3 genres of music (rap, classical, pop, etc) or songs that they would bring with them in their treasure trunk on a journey to another country.

5.) Scan through the musical suggestions and find several pieces that fit in these genres to listen to for the next class. Have students listen for similarities and differences in each type of music.

6.) Design a map of where the class would like to travel and what music they would play at each place. Then, have them decide what things or music they would bring back with them. Place these ideas into their treasure trunk.

7.) Review the items in the trunk and discuss how people bring new ideas and items with them as they travel the world.

Travel Mix

Assessment:

Create an iPod travel mix of the music from student "travels" during your lesson. Students can then create a music map that shows what music is added in each location along with a narrative of one place that they "visited".

Introduction

This lesson seed combines Common Core literature reading standards and visual art standards. It's so incredible how many ELA Common Core Standards you can meet when using an Arts Integration lesson – it really is a time-saver! This lesson pairs Robinson Crusoe and NC Wyeth's illustrations to explore point of view, illustration technique, and synthesis of text. This has been written for Grade 4, and the text complexity of the selected chapter conveys this new sense of rigor and the materials are all hyperlinked for you. There's even an extension to compare the works of NC, Andrew and Jamie Wyeth through a research project, which can be connected to the corresponding writing standards for 4th grade. This rich lesson seed will provide you with a great way to engage your students while pushing their boundaries in literature.

Grade Level: 4-6

Additional Materials (located in Appendix B): Puzzle, Think, Explore Sheet, NC Wyeth Illustration Link

Standards:

Common Core	Fine Arts
CCSS.ELA-Literacy.RL.4.1 Refer to details and examples in a text when explaining what the text says explicitly and when drawing inferences from the text. CCSS.ELA-Literacy.RL.4.2 Determine a theme of a story, drama, or poem from details in the text; summarize the text. CCSS.ELA-Literacy.RL.4.3 Describe in depth a character, setting, or event in a story or drama, drawing on specific details in the text (e.g., a character's thoughts, words, or actions). CCSS.ELA-Literacy.RL.4.6 Compare and contrast the point of view from which different stories are narrated, including the difference between first- and third-person narrations. CCSS.ELA-Literacy.RL.4.7 Make connections between the text of a story or drama and a visual or oral presentation of the text, identifying where each version reflects specific descriptions and directions in the text.	Visual Art: Explain differences between and among historical, social, or cultural reasons for creating and using art, by studying artworks and other sources of information

Education Closet

lesson seeds

READING THE *Art*

COMMON CORE READING AND VISUAL ART

Objectives

CONTENT	FINE ARTS
CCSS.ELA Literacy.RL. 4.1, 4.2, 4.3, 4.6, 4.7	Visual Art: Explain differences between and among historical, social, or cultural reasons for creating and using art, by studying artworks and other sources of information

Materials:

Illustration #13 by NC Wyeth

Robinson Crusoe Chapter 27 excerpt

paper, pencils, tablet, etc.

Watercolor paper and paints.

Extensions:

Compare the art of NC Wyeth to that of his son, Andrew and grandson Jamie. How do each of these artists share a story? What elements are the same and different in how they share their point of view?

1. Students visually study Robinson Crusoe Illustration No. 13 by NC Wyeth using this Puzzle, Think, Explore technique. Create a categorized list of student responses.
2. Ask students to now look at the colors, light and dark shading, and textures of the print and summarize this scene from the point of view of the Captain. Then, have them do the same thing from the point of view of Robinson Crusoe.
3. Provide students with an excerpt from Robinson Crusoe for Chapter 27. Ask them to read the selection carefully to find any comparisons between the text description and their previous ideas of the scene based on the illustration.
4. Compare the textual nuances of phrasing, word choice, and voice to the use of shading, textures and color used in the illustration. Do they match? How so? How does the illustration capture the feeling of the text? Provide an opportunity for students to compare and contrast in small groups these (and other) questions of inquiry.
5. Groups can present their findings to the whole class and engage in a discussion on the similarities and differences between the text and the illustration in capturing the scene.
6. Have students reflect on how reading printed text and reading a visual art print are the same and different and what decoding techniques you need to use for each source.

Assessment:

Alternate Point of View

Robinson Crusoe is told from the point of view of Robinson himself. Have students re-write the selection they read from the point of view of the captain and then sketch an illustration that utilizes texture, color and shading to support and convey the captain's point of view of this moment.

Introduction

This lesson seed uses some drama techniques and extends and engages students within their social studies curriculum. Notice that the Common Core Standard is from the Literacy Standards for Technical Subjects. This lesson seed is focused on the pivotal event of the Civil War. It provides students with the opportunities to research this historical moment in time, as well as the generals who were instrumental in that event. They conclude with interviews of these generals.

Grade Level: 6-8

Standards

Common Core	Fine Arts
CCSS.ELA-Literacy.RH.6-8.6 Identify aspects of a text that reveal an author's point of view or purpose (e.g., loaded language, inclusion or avoidance of particular facts).	Drama: Students can use the tools of acting to immerse themselves within a character.

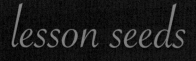

lesson seeds
THE GENERAL'S *interview*

S O C I A L   S T U D I E S   A N D   D R A M A

Objectives

CONTENT	FINE ARTS
Social Studies: Students can understand and describe historical events and their impact. CCSS.ELA-Literacy.RH.6-8.6	**Drama**: Students can use the tools of acting to immerse themselves within a character.

Materials:

* Computer, LCD projector, Internet

* Photos from the American Civil War

* News articles on current world events/ civil wars

* News articles from 1865

* Paper, pencils

Extensions:

Create a press conference for Grant and Lee visiting the world today and their commentary on world events and civil wars happening in Egypt and Libya today.

1.) Students read several archived newspapers on the current world unrest (Ghadaffi, Egypt, Afghanistan, Iraq) to gain understanding of current world events. Discuss the Civil Wars that are currently going on in the world. What does Civil War mean? How is this different than a war between countries? Create a Venn Diagram comparing Civil War to War among countries.

2.) Then show students some pictures from the American Civil War. Narrate the pictures as you show them to create a personal history for each person (either real or imagined). Bring in pieces of what caused the Civil War into each narrative story. Example: "My name was Billy and my father owns a textile mill in Massachusetts, though now we produce boots for the North."

3.) Then, have students look at each picture, notice things about each person, background, or setting in the picture and create a narrative for what the people were thinking as the picture was being taken. Have students write these down.

4.) Have students conduct research on the causes of the American Civil War and the similarities and differences between that and the Civil Wars of today.

5.) Show students the picture of Lee and Grant at Appomattox Courthouse and repeat step 3 for only one of the men.

6.) Students get into pairs with one who wrote down what Lee was thinking and one who wrote down what Grant was thinking. Students then can compare their commentary. Finally, the teacher discusses what was really going on in the photograph and compares that to students' answers.

Assessment:

General Interviews
Have students create a town hall interview. One student is General Grant and the other is General Lee. There can be interviewers, townspeople, as many as you need. Have students interview the Generals on the surrender and what this means for America. Print the interviews into a class newspaper on the event.

Introduction

This lesson seed is all about concrete poetry and art. Concrete poetry is great for teaching because it connects both brain hemispheres immediately into one piece of art. You really can reach all children at some level with concrete poetry. This lesson seed is geared more toward middle/high school students, but can be used with the younger grades with some modifications (which are included in the lesson). It's a neat little twist on an old artform, along with using the geometric artwork of Betty Halwey Kelso. By the time you're through with this lesson, students will have worked through geometry, measurement, poetry and visual art objectives all at the same time.

Grade Level: 6-9

Additional Materials (found in Appendix B): I See, I Think, I Wonder Chart

Standards

Common Core	Fine Arts
CCSS.ELA-Literacy.RL.6.4: Determine the meaning of words and phrases as they are used in a text, including figurative and connotative meanings; analyze the impact of a specific word choice on meaning and tone	Art: Students can observe and critique famous artists and styles. Students can create a piece of art using a specified artistic technique.
CCSS.ELA-Literacy.RL.6.7: Compare and contrast the experience of reading a story, drama, or poem to listening to or viewing an audio, video, or live version of the text, including contrasting what they "see" and "hear" when reading the text to what they perceive when they listen or watch.	
CCSS.ELA-Literacy.W.6.9a: Apply *grade 6 Reading standards* to literature (e.g., "Compare and contrast texts in different forms or genres [e.g., stories and poems; historical novels and fantasy stories] in terms of their approaches to similar themes and topics").	
CCSS Math 6.G.3, 6.G.4: Draw polygons in the coordinate plane given coordinates for the vertices; Apply these techniques in the context of solving real-world and mathematical problems.	

lesson seeds
THE SHAPE shifter
P O E T R Y ,   M A T H   A N D   A R T

Objectives

CONTENT	FINE ARTS
Reading: CCSS.ELA-Literacy.RL.6.4, CCSS.ELA-Literacy.RL.6.7 CCSS.ELA-Literacy.W.6.9a **Math:** CCSS 6.G.3, 6.G.4	**Art**: Students can observe and critique famous artists and styles. Students can create a piece of art using a specified artistic technique.

Materials:

* **LCD Projector, Computer, Internet**

* **Rulers**

* Construction paper, paint, paintbrushes, pencils, markers

* poems (listed in lesson)

* Betty Hawley Keslo prints

Extensions:

Create a class shape mosaic by cutting up each piece of shape art/poetry and putting it together within the confines of a geometric shape

1.) Have students look at art samples online by Betty Hawley Kelso. Have them create a see, think, wonder chart (I see... I think....I wonder....) comparing her various works using geometric abstract art. Discuss if the design was purposeful, the color choices, if measurement might have been involved, etc.

2.) Then, have students do the same activity with Shape Poetry. Using the example of Old Mazda Lamp (grades 7+) or The Giraffe (grades 1-5 - Located in "Where the Sidewalk Ends"), show students the artistic way that some poets write their stories: as the shapes of which they are describing.

3.) Compare writing about the qualities of a shape to drawing a picture using these shapes together. What is the same? What is different? What skills are needed to do both activities? Create a list of these skills.

4.) Give students a copy of a Kelso painting. Have them measure various shapes using rulers to see if each shape is in proportion to the other, and if the measurements are exact. Discuss their findings as a class. What did this mean from the artistic point of view? From the math point of view?

5.) Have students create a Kelso painting using squares, triangles, circles, and rectangles only. The shapes must be measured exactly and the final picture must be of an item that they could write about.

6.) Students then write a poem within their geometric painting that describes the qualities or meaning of that shape without naming it.

Assessment:

Assess for accuracy, creativity, and development!
Create a rubric that you share with students for this assessment that tells them how many shapes to use, what types of shapes, looks for measurement accuracy and looks for the use of allegory in their shape poem. Have students grade themselves and then grade it from a teaching perspective. Combine the two grades for the final assessment.

Introduction

This lesson seed addresses music, dance, drama, theatre, literature and math. The inspiration for this lesson came by speaking with a teacher from North Carolina. She is facing what a lot of teachers are facing right now: the reality of teaching classes that she doesn't specialize in. With cutbacks in teachers, materials, and funding, we are all being asked to teach more than ever before. This wonderful teacher explained that she was a drama teacher by trade, but was being asked to integrate music into her curriculum. To address this common dilemma, this lesson seed was created to authentically teach many contents and is a project-based unit rather than just a simple lesson seed.

Grade Level: 7-9

Standards

Common Core	Fine Arts
CCSS.ELA-Literacy.RL.7.2 Determine a theme or central idea of a text and analyze its development over the course of the text; provide an objective summary of the text.	Music: Students can demonstrate understanding and use of meter.
CCSS.ELA-Literacy.RL.7.5 Analyze how a drama's or poem's form or structure (e.g., soliloquy, sonnet) contributes to its meaning	Drama: Students can use dramatic interactions to tell a story.
CCSS.ELA-Literacy.RL.7.9 Compare and contrast a fictional portrayal of a time, place, or character and a historical account of the same period as a means of understanding how authors of fiction use or alter history.	
CCSS Math 7.NS.1 Apply and extend previous understandings of addition and subtraction to add and subtract rational numbers	

Education Closet

lesson seeds

WEST SIDE *shifts*

M A T H , M U S I C , D R A M A , L I T E R A T U R E

Objectives

CONTENT	FINE ARTS
Literature: Common Core RL 7.2, 7.5, 7.9 **Math**: Common Core 7.NS.1	**Music**: Students can demonstrate understanding and use of meter. **Drama**: Students can use dramatic interactions to tell a story.

Materials:

* DVD/CD of West Side Story

* Scripts of Romeo and Juliet

* Journals

* Pencils

* Music from "America"

Extensions:

* Record each dance and create a movie collage.

* Create a Wordle of similarities between WSS and Romeo/Juliet

1.) Have the students read through a portion of the script from West Side Story and the comparable portion of Romeo and Juliet and create Venn Diagrams of what is similar and different to both.

2.) Listen to the song "America" from WSS. It's all about hopes and dreams for the future and the importance of possibility. Students could relate this back to themselves and their own hopes and dreams. Have each student keep a list of these things in their own personal journals.

3.) Talk about how the music from the song switches meter - it goes from 4/4 time to 3/4 and then back again. This was done for a couple of reasons. Leonard Bernstein (the composer) wanted the song to both tell a story and be used as a traditional hispanic dance piece. The 3/4 allows for the dance and the 4/4 allows for the story. The other reason that Bernstein wrote it this way was because he wanted to juxtapose the feeling of freedom (3/4) with the structure of daily life (4/4). Use this as a starting off point for students to discover meter and how changing a meter can immediately change the feel and meaning of the music.

4.) Have students form groups and assign them either 4/4 or 3/4. Each group must design 4 measures of dance choreography in their assigned meter (3 steps or 4).

5.) Play the music and have each group perform their dance during their assigned meter. This way, you can assess whether or not they can hear the shift in meter and understand the groupings of 3 or 4 by watching their steps.

Assessment:

Students brainstorm a different storyline for their own "possibility" piece by using the ideas they wrote down in their journals within their small groups. This can be a monologue before the "America" piece. Have each small group act out their monologues and perform their "America" dances as a culminating activity. Use a rubric to grade both objectives.

Introduction

This lesson seed shares how to use the Stippling technique as a way to convert graphical data into meaningful context. This lesson has been designed using 7th grade Common Core math standards for statistics, as well as 7th grade visual arts standards. Plus, the lesson has been developed keeping the STEM practices in mind, so this could very easily be turned into a full-blown STEAM lesson, should you so choose.

Grade Level: 7-9
Additional Materials (found in Appendix B): Stippling Technique

Standards

Common Core	Fine Arts
CCSS Math 7.RP.2.b Identify the constant of proportionality (unit rate) in tables, graphs, equations, diagrams, and verbal descriptions of proportional relationships. 7.RP.2.d Explain what a point (x, y) on the graph of a proportional relationship means in terms of the situation, with special attention to the points (0, 0) and (1, r) where r is the unit rate. 7.SP.1 Understand that statistics can be used to gain information about a population by examining a sample of the population; generalizations about a population from a sample are valid only if the sample is representative of that population. Understand that random sampling tends to produce representative samples and support valid inferences. 7.SP.2 Use data from a random sample to draw inferences about a population with an unknown characteristic of interest. Generate multiple samples (or simulated samples) of the same size to gauge the variation in estimates or predictions.	Visual Art: Demonstrate understanding of processes for solving visual problems

lesson seeds
STIPPLING *graphs*

STATISTICS AND VISUAL ART

Objectives

CONTENT	FINE ARTS
Common Core Math: 7.RP.2.b, 7.RP.2.d, 7.SP.1, 7.SP.2	Visual Art:Demonstrate understanding of processes for solving visual problems

Materials:

•Internet access: http:// gapminder.org/ world

•Computers

•Graphing paper

•Markers of varying width and colors

1. Begin by using Gapminder.org/world and select "Open Graph Menu". As a class, explore some of graphs based on questions students would like to know more about.

2. Guide students in how to read a graph and what the colors and sizes of the dots indicate on GapMinder (ie: the larger the dot and the warmer the color, the higher the percentage or number).

3. Have students each create a question that they would like to explore more deeply, using the ones on GapMinder as an example.

4. Have students spend one class period researching as much as they can on their chosen question and write down their findings in report format.

5. Translate those findings onto a paper graph using standard graphing techniques and measurements (being sure to include labels).

6. Create a Stipple artwork on the graph using Stippling Techniques with color, proximity and size of the dots to indicate the importance of the findings.

Assessment:

Graphique Critique
Provide students with a scoring rubric that outlines both the elements of the graph you want to see, as well as the elements of the Stippling technique they need to have included. Give each student one rubric to score themselves and another rubric to score a peer. On the peer review, include a section where they can write what they have learned based on the stippled graph from their classmate.

Introduction

In this lesson seed, students will get the opportunity to explore one of the signers of the Declaration of Independence before the day arrived and become an advocate for their own positions. The Hot-Seat technique (explained in the assessment section) is used during the Class Congress as a way to explore these variables in more detail and as a way for students to truly feel what it might have been like in that hot room on July 1st. Written for high school students, this lesson correlates 10th grade Speaking and Listening Common Core Standards with Drama processes to produce a fascinating account of what could have been in 1776.

Grade Level: 9-12

Additional Materials (found in Appendix B): John Adams' Speech

Standards

Common Core	Fine Arts
CCSS.ELA-Literacy.RL.9-10.1 Cite strong and thorough textual evidence to support analysis of what the text says explicitly as well as inferences drawn from the text. CCSS.ELA-Literacy.RL.9-10.3 Analyze how complex characters (e.g., those with multiple or conflicting motivations) develop over the course of a text, interact with other characters, and advance the plot or develop the theme. CCSS.ELA-Literacy.SL.9-10.1a Come to discussions prepared, having read and researched material under study; explicitly draw on that preparation by referring to evidence from texts and other research on the topic or issue to stimulate a thoughtful, well-reasoned exchange of ideas. CCSS.ELA-Literacy.SL.9-10.1c Propel conversations by posing and responding to questions that relate the current discussion to broader themes or larger ideas; actively incorporate others into the discussion; and clarify, verify, or challenge ideas and conclusions.	Drama: Select a variety of sources, e.g. original ideas, fictional or non-fictional works, theatrical structures, and theatrical elements to create and produce dramatic works.

lesson seeds
FOUNDERS *drama*

LANGUAGE ARTS AND DRAMA

Objectives

CONTENT	FINE ARTS
Common Core Reading: <u>RL.9-10.1</u>, <u>RL. 9-10.3</u>, <u>SL.9-10.1a</u>, <u>SL.9-10.1c</u>	Drama: Select a variety of sources, e.g. original ideas, fictional or non-fictional works, theatrical structures, and theatrical elements to create and produce dramatic works.

Materials:

• Computers

• Journals

• Pens/Paper/Pencils

• John Adams' Speech (linked in the lesson)

• Classroom setup as a Continental Congress would be.

• Period dress (if you choose)

1. Start by assigning each student in the class a historical figure from the Continental Congress to "become". Explain that they will be researching this person and their backgrounds in great detail. The teacher will be John Adams.

2. Using guided internet search and informational texts from the library, facilitate student research of their assigned characters. Have them focus on the following items: family, religious beliefs, time that they lived, what they ate, any special talents they had, and where they stood on the issue of Independence as of July 1st, 1776.

3. The teacher should also memorize the arguments as outlined in <u>John Adams' speech</u> to the gathering on July 1st when he swayed many of them to declare independence.

4. Students should then develop arguments for their position on independence and be prepared to speak in front of the class congress.

5. Set up a class congress and allow each student to speak for their position for up to 5 minutes. Encourage other students to ask questions and refute other students' speeches when giving their own.

6. After the class has finished their own debate on the merits of declaring independence, based on true-life accounts of their characters, the teacher will stand up as John Adams and give a speech trying to persuade the other characters to sign a Declaration of Independence, using the actual speech as a basis for this 5-minute argument.

Assessment:

A Journal through Time

Many of the founding fathers kept journals to document the history of the time. Ask students to write in their own journals as if they are still in character about whether or not to sign the Declaration and what John Adams' speech may have done to influence their decision.

Introduction

This STEAM lesson seed focuses on one of the hottest topics to our students (and let's face it…ourselves): which cell phone is better? The iPhone 5 or the Samsung GIII? Using this topic, we ask students why certain apps work better on one of these phones over the other? Their task: to design a platform for their chosen phone that will allow all apps to function optimally. Additionally, they must design and create an advertising campaign using the elements of design to communicate their message effectively and lure customers to switch to their phone. Designed for students in Grades 7-12, this lesson is an exciting way to integrate across all disciplines.

Grade Level: 7-12
Standards

Common Core	Fine Arts
STEM 2.A. Analyze interdisciplinary connections that exist within science, technology, engineering, and mathematics disciplines and other disciplines. STEM 2.B. Apply integrated science, technology, engineering, mathematics content, and other content as appropriate to answer complex questions, to investigate global issues, and to develop solutions for challenges and real world problems. STEM 3.C. Engage in critical reading and writing of technical information. STEM 3.F. Communicate effectively and precisely with others.	Visual Art: Demonstrate how media, processes, and techniques communicate ideas and personal meaning

Education Closet

lesson seeds

MOBILE *Battles*

STEM AND DESIGN

Objectives

CONTENT	FINE ARTS
STEM Practices 2.A, 2.B, 3.C, 3.F	Visual Art:Demonstrate how media, processes, and techniques communicate ideas and personal meaning

Materials:

Consumer Reports for iPhone 5 and Samsung G3 phones

Print advertisements for both phones

Video advertisements for both phones

Computers, Internet, paper and pencils, design software

Video camera

1. Students will watch and read advertisements for the Samsung GIII cell phone and the Apple iPhone 5. Use a variety of video and print advertisements.

2. Have students prepare a 3 minute debate for why one of the cell phones is better than the other. Students must cite at least 3 sources of research for their 3 minute presentations.

3. After holding the debate, discuss why people may prefer one platform over the other, even after having all of the information to make an informed decision.

4. Have students make a list of their favorite apps as a class. Then, ask them to choose one of the apps from the list. Ask them "What phone platform will allow your app to perform at its optimum level?" (this is a major point of contention in the current battles between the two phones. Select apps perform better on one or the other platform. IE: pandora works better with iPhone and iHeartRadio works better with the SG3)

5. Students must research through consumer reports or their own action research which phone works better for their chosen app. They must then prepare an infographic that synthesizes what they learned.

6. Students can work in collaborative teams (based on apps that worked best on the same platform - eg: all apps that work well on iPhone 5) to design a solution that would allow better functionality of the other apps for their chosen device. Students must use the elements of design within their approach for the platform, as well as for their advertisements to promote their designed solution.

Assessment:

Advertisement

Students will create a marketing campaign of 1 print and 1 (30 second) video that promotes their design solution for their cell phone. They must use the elements of design in their creations, with the intention that their advertisements are creative and innovative to lure customers away from their current phones.

Part 3: Assessments

part
_____
THREE

An Assessment Culture

We are obsessed with assessments in education. We want to know how much a student knows, what they know, when they knew it and who is to blame if they don't know what they are supposed to know when they are supposed to know it.

But what does knowing mean?

When working through an integrated lesson, one of the first things you'll notice is the breadth and depth of knowledge that your students have and their innate ability to transfer that knowledge across topics. This process of transfer and application is just as critical to assess as the ability to retain and demonstrate skill mastery. All are a part of knowing and as such, we must have a way to assess them all.

Speaking of assessment, it is also crucial that we are all operating under the same definition of this term. Assessment is not the same as evaluation. Evaluation is about making judgments. It's about staking a claim that the work is either good or bad, correct or incorrect, this or that. Assessment is none of those things. Assessment is a measurement of growth so far. It is not finite, nor does it place a specific judgment of "rightness". Instead, it helps us to monitor where students are in their learning journey in comparison to both themselves and to their peers.

This working definition of assessment seems to put a lot of teachers at ease when they begin to practice integrated lesson planning and implementation. Often, this assessment piece is the part that holds many teachers back. You'll hear them say things like "I'm can't assess that subject - I'm not qualified" or "Why do I have to assess that standard? It's not my area of expertise" and this is a very valid concern...if we were talking about evaluation. But we're not. We're not asking teachers to make a qualified judgment about student skill, ability or talent in a subject area that is not their area of certification or expertise. Rather, we're asking them to measure student growth or rate of progress towards meeting a naturally aligned set of standards across subjects. The measurement is in comparison to both their peers and their previous work, for which any teacher is qualified to assess. The technical skills, competencies and artistry that other subjects teach should and are assessed within those classrooms. But the growth in and appropriate use of these core components to connect with other standards can be assessed in multiple settings.

Types of Assessments

There are four main types of assessments that we will focus on in this book:

- Summative
- Formative
- Portfolio
- Performance

Can you guess which one of those is the most widely used and accepted form of assessment in American Education today? Of course you can - Summative Assessments. Those so-called "high stakes" tests which ask students to answer yes or no, if/then, right or wrong questions. These are the tests that tell us if our schools are successful or failing, if our students are advance, proficient or basic in their knowledge, and if our teachers are outstanding or incompetent, if you believe the bill of goods that many testing companies are trying to sell. However, we know that Summative Assessments cannot possibly tell us everything there is to know about the growth, ability, and future success of any child. It is a snapshot from one day - good or bad - that places a number on that child's performance.

Why do we continue to use summative assessments then, if we know that they are ineffective in measuring what we are truly seeking in terms of student achievement? Because they are consistent and standardized. There is no variation, no way for teacher or evaluator bias to enter into the mix. And there are times when summative assessments are appropriate. They are certainly part of the package that tells us about student learning.

There are some things about all subjects and contents that are either right or wrong, and you either know them or you don't. In these instances, it is absolutely fine to provide a summative assessment to gain insight into what students know about pure information, inferencing ability, and problem-solving. Even in integrated lessons, there are times when we need to have a measure of what basic skills and information our students understand so that we can have them apply these skills and transfer this information later on. All of this is to say, however, that summative assessments are a very small part of the assessment package that we need to use in integrated studies to measure student growth and achievement.

A New Focus

This book will set aside the discussion of summative assessments in order to delve more deeply into the other three assessment formats. Please do not interpret this to mean that summative assessments are not valued in integrated studies. This is not true at all. Certainly, there are times when multiple choice, open response, true and false and other summative assessments are the appropriate choice to measure student understanding. However, because integrated studies - particularly STEM and Arts Integration - focus on bringing two or more naturally aligning standards together to teach in and through two content areas, assessing these standards authentically can be challenging and summative assessments may not offer the flexibility and comprehensive picture that these other formats provide.

This section is divided into the remaining three assessment types: Formative, Portfolio and Performance. Each is explored in depth and has practical samples and templates for you to use in integrated lessons. Please know that these are not the only tools that are available to you, but they will provide you with a good start in assessing multiple content areas with integrity.

Finally, before we move on to these three assessment formats, it is sometimes helpful to see an organized list of assessment tools that are available as a reminder of the many ways that we can critically measure student growth over time and their achievement of mastery. The Integrated Assessment Pinboard on the following page provides you with a list of ideas for strategies you can use to assess student understanding, application and presentation. Some of these are large-scale items and some are things you can do tomorrow. Keep this list handy as you are planning to remember that you don't have to get stuck in a rut when it comes to assessment. Mix it up and find what works for you!

Integration Assessment Pinboard

Assessment Strategies Profile

These assessment strategies are suggested tools for measuring growth in selected content areas. This is far from a comprehensive list, but does give you ideas for authentic assessment design.

These strategies connect with:

- Common Core Math

- Common Core Language Arts

- Additional Core Contents

- 21st Century Skills

Common Core Math

Skill Mastery

- Multiple Choice
- Short Answer
- Visual Representation
- Fill in the Blank
- Models

Use of Practices

- Project-based learning (architecture, design, simulation)
- Movement sequences
- Composition
- Process descriptions/drawing
- Product Development

Common Core Language Arts

Reading and Language

- Notation and Symbols
- Use of Vocabulary
- Rhythmic Read-Alouds
- Staircasing Complex Pieces for Reading (music, art, dances, plays)

Writing and Speaking and Listening

- Plays and Skits
- Musical Phrases
- Debates and Enactments
- Choreographed Dance
- Visual Thinking

Media Technology

- Tweet/140 character synthesis statement
- Blog post
- Wall post
- Ignite! Presentation
- App presentation

Additional Core Contents:
Science, Social Studies, Technical, Fine Arts

Skill Mastery

- Interactive Poll
- Article
- Data Analysis
- Performance
- Composition
- Rubric

Relationship to Context

- Integrated project
- STEM project
- Gaming
- Research and presentation of findings

Application and Critique

- Design (costumes, scenery, skits, music, art)
- Build Websites
- Improvisation
- Peer reviews
- Analysis of master work

21st Century Skills

The 4 C's: Creativity, Collaboration, Critical Thinking, Communication

- Tableau
- Investigations
- Hot-Seating
- Business partnerships/internships
- Wiki entries/Journal entries
- Online Portfolios

Literacy Across Subjects

- Reading non-traditional texts (music, art, choreography)
- Sliderocket, Prezi and other Presentations
- Using web-based tools

Formative Assessments

Formative assessments are key components in the overall picture of student performance. Often, we are so concerned with summative assessments, or concrete evidence that we skip over "checking in" with students as they go through the process of learning. Formative assessments provide us with essential knowledge as facilitators of the components that our students are struggling with, as well as those over which they have a firm grasp. These assessments should take place frequently, and are generally observational in their format. Often, when fine arts teacher assess students, it is mainly through formative assessment with the summative assessment being reserved for the finished work. So if you are hesitant about assessing students in an integrated area, such as the Arts or STEM, because you do not have training in that content, don't worry! Formative assessments are a valuable and integral part of any integrated lesson.

In this short section, I am sharing with you 6 of my favorite formative assessment strategies. There are literally hundreds of formative assessments out there that you can use, and links to a selected variety of them can be found below. Please use these links and the featured 6 strategies on these pages as starting points for you to explore the amazing possibilities for gauging student work that exist!

 STEM Assessments: http://bit.ly/QWfseZ

 Project Zero Visible Thinking Routines: http://bit.ly/RRydNP

 WVDE Teach21: http://bit.ly/UdjLC0

 Formative Assessment: Examples of Practice (E. Caroline Wylie): http://bit.ly/Y00y9G

Video/Audio Log

Video or Audio logs are a great way to provide instant feedback to students. You can record your feedback through free applications like Jing or Quicktime and email them to students or place them on a wiki/blog page. These guiding questions will help frame what you are looking for in their work and insights you may have. Additionally, this log could be used for peer feedback as well!

Directions: View the selected presentation or work. Record your feedback via video or audio

Guiding Questions	Comments/Thoughts
Did the student address the topic that was assigned? Why or why not?	
What evidence of student learning and understanding do you see in this work?	
What was the student's biggest challenge in working through this project?	
What are your primary concerns about the student's performance in meeting the challenges of this project?	
What elements of the student's work are you most proud of?	
What are the next steps for this student based on their performance on this project?	

STEAM Statements

STEAM Statements are writings that communicate the synthesis of a student's work. They may be used to describe the basis for the work, why it was chosen, what the student is hoping to communicate and the purpose of the piece. The Authentic Integrated Rubric may be used as a standard measure for assessment in STEAM Statements.

STEAM Statement Elements:

1. After students complete their work and have prepared their presentation, they will create a STEAM Statement to accompany their work.

2. These statements are short - one to three paragraphs is preferred.

3. STEAM Statements should use language that is appropriate to the intended audience.

4. These Statements address the following questions:

    a. Why did you create this work?

    b. What does this work signify?

    c. How did you create this piece/solution?

    d. What is the work made of (if applicable)?

    e. What does this work mean to you?

5. Statements provide readers with the option to agree or disagree with the work. This provides a deeper learning experience for everyone.

6. STEAM Statements are as specific as possible.

7. The Statements are compelling and provide the reader with a desire to learn more about the work.

The Spinning Wheel

The Spinning Wheel is a formative assessment activity that allows students to provide each other with quick feedback from multiple sources. If they hear the same feedback through each round, it's an easy indication that they need to go back and revise their work. Additionally, teachers can get a quick handle on student understanding of key concepts by listening to their students as they facilitate the activity. **Be sure to provide students with 2-3 key ideas they are looking for when reviewing another student's work.**

Directions:

1. Divide the class in half.

2. The first half of the class forms a circle facing outward, holding their work in front of them.

3. The second half of the class forms a circle around the outside of the first circle. Each student in the outside circle should be facing someone on the inside circle. The outside circle will also hold their work in front of them.

4. When the teacher says "Go" students on the outside circle will have 30 seconds to explain their work to their inside circle partner. The inside circle partner will then have 30 seconds to provide feedback on the work they just heard about.

5. At the end of one minute, the teacher will say "Rotate". The outside circle will rotate clockwise while the inside circle stays still. Now, each student has a different partner.

6. Repeat steps 4 and 5 until everyone has seen everyone else's work.

7. Students may then return to their workspace to make revisions based on peer reviews.

Hot Seating

Hot-seating requires deep understanding of a subject, and the ability to improvise while at the same time remaining within character. Essentially, hot-seating is when the teacher or student takes a role and students may ask that "character" any questions they would like. The person within the character must know many details about that character, the time period, societal background and economic drivers in order to accurately portray that character. And the students asking the questions must think of questions that would be appropriate to those circumstance as well. Teachers can use this as a way quickly assess current knowledge on a topic, as well as depth of understanding of context.

Directions:

1. Choose a a list of characters from a piece of literature or a time period that you are currently studying.

2. Provide selected students one of these characters to study and portray using a selected topic (ie: civil liberties, equality, taxes, etc).

3. Ask the other students who do not have a character to research the time period and circumstances. They may interpret this research through the lens of a variety of perspectives (ie: journalist, citizen, teacher, doctor, etc). These students should develop specific questions for each character based on their research and from their chosen perspective.

4. Have each character briefly begin by introducing themselves, providing some background knowledge and what their beliefs are on the current topic of discussion.

5. Students may then ask each character questions based on their research and engage the characters in a discussion based on their responses. The responses must be based in only the knowledge and circumstances of the time period with which you are working.

Obviously, this can make connections to many different contents, but most specifically social studies and the research element of Common Core reading and writing. Students must be able to read rigorous non-fiction texts, look for multiple sources, and develop arguments based on their research. You could also weave math and science fairly seamlessly into this if looking at the economics or scientific advancements of the time period you selected.

Deck of Cards

The Deck of Cards activity is another way to use formative assessment in a fun, low-threatening way for students. This allows for student choice and can be used in short bursts during the progress of work, rather than at the end. As you are working on a project, use this activity to help students work through the revision process to help refine their work and develop their supporting details.

Directions:

1. Provide each student with a single card from a deck of cards.

2. Explain to the students that they will only receive one card and that card is precious. They may only give it away if they see something special that they would like to know more about.

3. Have each student lay their work in progress out on their desk or table.

4. Tell students that they will walk around the room examining each others' work. If they find a piece of work that looks interesting, or that they want to hear more about, they should place their card on that piece of work. If they do not see anything they are interested in, they should keep their card and place it on their own piece of work.

5. At the end of the exploration, the students with the most cards on their work will each have 1-2 minutes to explain what they are working on and what they are planning to do next. Students who placed their cards on that work may ask one follow-up question or provide one feedback statement.

Tableau

Tableau is a powerful tool that can be used with students of all ability levels. From special needs students to gifted/talented students, all children can use this method to demonstrate their learning.

Tableau is simply a frozen picture of a moment in time. These are another "low risk" vehicle for arts integration. Teachers are not asked to do things which are uncomfortable and students love to stretch their imaginations with this task.

Directions:

1. Each student chooses something from the story to "be". For instance, in the book I'll Love You Forever, there is a page that talks about the boy when he is 9 years old and walking through the house. One student might be the boy, one might be the sink with dirty dishes, one might be his backpack on the floor.

2. Have students think about ALL the elements in this one scene. They should pick things that are at all levels – low (floor, items on the ground), medium (things that are at eye level) or high (what is happening above the main object).

3. Give students just a few seconds (no more than a minute) to decide what their tableau will look like and tell or ask them to think about which drama tools to activate: body, imagination, concentration or collaboration.

4. When the teacher says "Action!" student groups will all freeze in their tableaus. This is the moment that you will first assess the assignment. Did students choose an element of consequence and use an appropriate tool to demonstrate their understanding?

5. Then, the teacher will highlight a group with a spotlight. When the spotlight is on a group, the teacher can ask each object/character what they are and what they think about the current scene as that character. This the second way you can assess student learning – by what and how they are describing their point of view as part of the story.

Portfolio Assessment

Using portfolios as a way to assess student work has been around a long time. Yet, they haven't really started to share the assessment spotlight until recently. That's because we have finally reached a point where we can use technology to support the structure of portfolios, making it a much more realistic avenue to assess student learning.

A student-selected portfolio contains a much more thorough and rich assessment of real student achievement. These portfolios contain specified pieces of work (as outlined by the teacher through the use of a rubric) that the student chooses and collects over a given period of time. They can be used for differentiation and inclusion and are truly a means for assessing everyone. The teacher can then use these portfolios in a variety of ways to assess student learning:

1.) Through a conference with the student. Teachers and students can go over the portfolios together and go through the rubric to see if students met the achievement standard. This provides a way for students to visually see their own progress, take ownership of their work and for the teacher to get to know the student's strengths and weaknesses through a variety of samples.

2.) Through a conference with the parents. Teachers and parents can go over the portfolios at their quarterly conference to get a better idea of how fast/slow a student is progressing, as a comparison to the mean progression rate, and as a way for parents to visually see what kind of work their child is doing in relationship to the areas they are studying. These portfolios can be presented by the student, or by the teacher depending on the situation.

3.) As a way to assess a project. Throughout the project, students can keep work samples in their portfolios and have a compilation of information and assignments at the end of a project that can be measured against a rubric for achievement standards. This is particularly helpful in an arts integration lesson when teachers are at a loss for how to assess the fine arts objectives with the content objectives.

Student portfolios are a wonderful way to assess true student knowledge and connections beyond the content. On the next two pages, you will find a sample Portfolio Assessment Rubric and a template that you can use to create one with your own components. I encourage you to consider this type of performance assessment when developing your assessment strategy in integrated study.

Portfolio Assessment Rubric

Student Name: _____ Portfolio Topic: _____

Class: _____ Date: _____

Directions: Score each identified component based on completeness, attention to detail, accuracy, synthesis of ideas where appropriate, and inclusion of key elements.

Component	5 Excellent	4 Good	3 Average	2 Fair	1 Poor	Comments
Contains all identified essential items.						
Showcases a variety of work on key specified topics.						
Chosen artifacts reflect growth over time.						
Reflections/Critiques of work are included and demonstrate high quality craftsmanship.						
The student demonstrates an ability to connect multiple areas naturally throughout the portfolio.						
The portfolio is visually pleasing and easy to navigate.						
The portfolio uses multimedia purposefully to contribute an understanding of the overall body of work, its concepts, ideas and relationships.						
Writing conventions are adhered: citations are used as appropriate, grammatical errors are limited, and the writing effectively facilitates the student's communication of essential ideas and elements.						

Total Score: _____ / 40 = _____%

Exemplary: 90-100%   Proficient: 80-89%   Limited: 70-79%   Unsatisfactory: 69% or below

Portfolio Assessment Rubric

Student Name: _____ Portfolio Topic: _____

Class: _____ Date: _____

Directions: Score each identified component based on completeness, attention to detail, accuracy, synthesis of ideas where appropriate, and inclusion of key elements.

Component	5 Excellent	4 Good	3 Average	2 Fair	1 Poor	Comments

Total Score: _____ / _____ = _____ %

Exemplary: 90-100%   Proficient: 80-89%   Limited: 70-79%   Unsatisfactory: 69% or below

Performance Assessment

Performance assessments are some of the most influential and exciting ways to authentically assess student work. This is because performance assessments look at a variety of components which reflect a total understanding of student knowledge, growth and application. Performance assessments provide in depth rubrics that measure conceptual knowledge, skill development, application and the performance itself. These assessments are the gold standard for many rigorous approaches, including STEM, IB (International Baccalaureate), 6+1 Writing, and Arts Integration (*see the References page for citations and links*). Additionally, while performance assessments provide a framework for use and rigorous standards of measurement, they also allow for flexibility in student interpretation, providing opportunities for multiple means of representation and expression - two of the hallmarks of Universal Design for Learning (http://www.cast.org/research/udl).

Performance assessments come with some challenges, however, that should be recognized before their implementation. Performance assessments are meant for long-term tasks and projects. This means that time will need to be provided for students to investigate, analyze, synthesize, collaborate and communicate their ideas in a variety of ways. This in turn signals that "traditional" classroom organization may not be appropriate for these tasks. Teachers release the role of lecturer and instead become facilitators, asking students probing questions on a topic, helping to guide them towards resources of value and framing their outcomes into relevant, manageable tasks. Both of these challenges: time and the transformation of a teacher's role will require professional development, patience and strong leadership to employ effectively. However, the benefits to this are tremendous. By using authentic performance assessments, students begin to control their own learning, thereby creating a culture of reflection, creativity, collaboration and critical thinking. All of these are key elements to 21st century education and performance assessments may assist in moving these critical needs forward into transformative practice.

In the following pages, you will find several highly-developed rubric systems that reflect an understanding of the latest recommendations from IB, PARCC, Universal Design for Learning, and 6+1 Writing in providing an integrated way to assess across content areas effectively and with authenticity. Let's get started.

Authentic Integration Assessment Rubric - Teacher Edition

Using the Teacher's Edition of the Authentic Integration Assessment

This edition of the assessment is meant for educator or administrator use. Each category listed provides a definition, as well as a scoring rubric and Enduring Understanding Question to ensure a rigorous, high-quality, consistent score for the selected work. This rubric may be used for a variety of topics and may span multiple contents as a connective assessment tool. Many areas may be assessed authentically with this tool, including:

- The Arts
- Writing
- STEM projects
- PYP/MYP/IB units of inquiry
- and any other project that intentionally links 2 or more topic areas

As with any tool, you must be cognizant of how and when you are using it to ensure its effectiveness. This assessment tool is not a "catch-all" when no other assessment seems to fit. It's intent is to be used to authentically measure a variety of elements in integrated study which naturally lend themselves to performance-based tasks.

The Authentic Integrated Assessment Rubric Structure

This rubric has 6 main components:

Concepts: Demonstrating an understanding and broad development of new ideas based in content knowledge.

Skills: Use of information to build capacity through deliberate, sustained effort.

Structure: Crafting the organization of a piece to share a clear point of view.

Development: The evolution of a piece through the editing process which demonstrates growth over time.

Application: The intentional transformation of skills and concepts into practice.

Presentation: A refined, finished work that synthesizes analytic thought, creative ideas, and a breadth of understanding of the relevant topic.

Additionally, there are **Enduring Understanding Questions** identified with each component to provide a singular idea that the component is trying to demonstrate. Why are these questions essential to the assessment process? Enduring Understanding Questions provide a synthesis of the larger picture of each component. By answering these questions, teachers and/or students are able to have a deep and meaningful comprehension of the component which transcends contents and makes lasting authentic connections.

How to Use the Authentic Integrated Assessment Rubric

There are a variety of ways to use this rubric effectively to measure student knowledge, growth and application. First, it's important to recognize that you do not need to measure all of the components all of the time. You may choose to measure only one or two of the components, depending on the standards you are measuring and the scope of the project itself. For example, if your students are working on an Arts Integration project that connects visual art and literacy standards, you may find that you would like to narrow your focus of assessment to Concepts and Application. This is perfectly acceptable, provided that you frame your lesson and project with those two components in mind.

The other way you can use this rubric is as a whole document that reflects all of the components you are looking for within a project. This is best used if your students are completing a large-scale project or challenge and you would like their assessment to reflect all of the ways in which they are demonstrating their knowledge, synthesis and sharing of a particular topic of study.

Scoring an Integrated Project using the Authentic Integrated Assessment Rubric

The overall rubric provided is divided into 3 main scores: 5 (exemplary) 3 (proficient) and 1 (limited). Beside each of these scores is an explanation or measurement that should match the student work you are scoring. If you would like to focus your scoring on one or two components, or if you are having difficulty in deciding between scores, the Focused Integrated Assessment Rubric may be a better reflection of student performance. Each component has a Focused Rubric that accompanies it, in which the component is further broken down into measurable areas. You may score each of these areas within the component, come up with a total score, which then determines the final score (5, 3 or 1) for that component.

In addition to your own score, there is an opportunity for student to score their own work with the Integrated Peer Review Sheet (discussed in the next section). You may use this score in a variety of ways which we will explore in the next section. Just keep in mind that this option is available to you and your students.

Remember to be as specific and consistent as possible when scoring student work. Often, it is recommended that teachers begin with using the Focused Integrated Assessment Rubric to calculate scores so as to attain that scoring consistency and to become comfortable with the elements of measure within each component. The next page contains the Teacher Scoring Rubric, as well as the accompanying Focused Integrated Assessment Rubrics for each component.

Authentic Integration Assessment Rubric - Teacher Edition

Concepts

Demonstrating an understanding and broad development of new ideas based in content knowledge.

5: The piece is clear and focused, makes meaningful connections and uses variations which enrich the central theme.

3: The theme of the piece is broad, with reasonably clear ideas and general observations.

1: The piece has no clear sense of purpose, is limited in its answer to a question and/or the theme is undeveloped.

Enduring Understanding Question: Is this piece focused and does it share original perspectives about a theme?

Skills

Use of information to build capacity through deliberate, sustained effort.

5: The student demonstrates in their work a wide range of relevant knowledge, uses sophisticated investigations and critical analysis, and their use of key elements are specific and accurate.

3: The work is functional, but lacks energy. The key elements are adequate in a general way.

1: The work demonstrates limited knowledge of key elements and does not convey specific meaning.

Enduring Understanding Question: Do the key elements used create a work that lingers in your mind?

Structure

Crafting the organization of a piece to share a clear point of view.

5: The student organizes information in a well-developed and logical sequence that connects ideas in a meaningful way.

3: The piece has a recognizable structure and is appropriate to the task, but the ideas are disconnected and distracting.

1: The structure of the piece is unclear and the composition is confusing, while the content is not relevant to the theme.

Enduring Understanding Question: Does the piece develop the ideas and theme to enhance the audience experience?

Development

The evolution of a piece through the editing process which demonstrates growth over time.

5: The piece has clearly been through multiple revisions and communicates a crafted vision that is succinct yet demonstrates great depth of understanding.

3: The piece has been through a revision and communicates a vision that is basic in its demonstration of understanding on the topic.

1: The piece has not been through an editing process and does not demonstrate any understanding over time.

Enduring Understanding Question: Does the work showcase the growth of student understanding over time?

Application

The intentional transformation of skills and concepts into practice.

5: The work reflects an ability to authentically connect multiple, relevant contents in a seamless way which demonstrates an extensive range of knowledge and skills.

3: The connections made to other subjects are forced or unclear; work demonstrates adequate knowledge of the topic.

1: There are no connections made across concepts; knowledge of topics is absent or superficial.

Enduring Understanding Question: Does the piece intentionally and naturally connect relevant information across subjects?

Presentation

A refined, finished work that synthesizes analytic thought, creative ideas, and a breadth of understanding of the relevant topic.

5: The piece is constructed in a way that underscores and enhances the meaning of the topic through purposeful use of key elements.

3: Parts of the piece invite expressive performance/presentation; others may be stiff, awkward or choppy.

1: This piece is choppy, incomplete or awkward. It does not clearly demonstrate the meaning of the topic.

Enduring Understanding Question: Does this presentation effectively and artistically communicate a clear interpretation of the topic?

www.educationcloset.com

Focused Authentic Integration Assessment Rubric

Student Name: _____   Task Focus: **Concepts**

Class: _____   Average Score: _____ / 30 = _____

Score Scale: 89-100% = 5   69-88% = 3   0-68% = 1

	5 Consistently demonstrates	4 Mostly demonstrates	3 Occasionally demonstrates	2 Demonstrates with assistance	1 Rarely demonstrates	0 Does not demonstrate
1. The chosen theme/idea is narrow and manageable.	5	4	3	2	1	0
2. Relevant, quality variations and details go beyond the obvious.	5	4	3	2	1	0
3. Ideas are crystal clear and supported with appropriate key elements.	5	4	3	2	1	0
4. The work demonstrates knowledge or experience.	5	4	3	2	1	0
5. The audience's natural questions are addressed and answered.	5	4	3	2	1	0
6. The ideas or theme is insightful, fresh and original.	5	4	3	2	1	0

Focused Authentic Integration Assessment Rubric

Student Name: _____ Task Focus: | **Skills** |

Class: _____ Average Score: _____ / 30 = _____

Score Scale: 89-100% = 5   69-88% = 3   0-68% = 1

	5	4	3	2	1	0
	Consistently demonstrates	Mostly demonstrates	Occasionally demonstrates	Demonstrates with assistance	Rarely demonstrates	Does not demonstrate
1. The basic elements and skills are generally correct, even on difficult tasks.	5	4	3	2	1	0
2. The use of elements and skills is accurate and guides the audience through the work.	5	4	3	2	1	0
3. A thorough understanding and consistent application of key skills is present.	5	4	3	2	1	0
4. Element useage contributes to the clarity of the work.	5	4	3	2	1	0
5. The student can manipulate the skills intentionally and it works well within the piece.	5	4	3	2	1	0
6. Precision is obvious.	5	4	3	2	1	0

Focused Authentic Integration Assessment Rubric

Student Name: _____ Task Focus: **Structure**

Class: _____ Average Score: _____ / 30 = _____

Score Scale: 89-100% = 5   69-88% = 3   0-68% = 1

	5 Consistently demonstrates	4 Mostly demonstrates	3 Occasionally demonstrates	2 Demonstrates with assistance	1 Rarely demonstrates	0 Does not demonstrate
1. The composition grabs the audience's attention and leaves them satisfied.	5	4	3	2	1	0
2. Movement through the piece connects ideas.	5	4	3	2	1	0
3. The arrangement of the composition is intentional and effective.	5	4	3	2	1	0
4. The piece meets the criteria that is set forth at the beginning of the lesson.	5	4	3	2	1	0
5. The piece is original and meets the theme.	5	4	3	2	1	0
6. The composition is purposeful and meaningful for the intended audience.	5	4	3	2	1	0

www.educationcloset.com

Focused Authentic Integration Assessment Rubric

Student Name: _____ Task Focus: **Development**

Class: _____ Average Score: ____ / 30 = _____

Score Scale: 89-100% = 5   69-88% = 3   0-68% = 1

	5 Consistently demonstrates	4 Mostly demonstrates	3 Occasionally demonstrates	2 Demonstrates with assistance	1 Rarely demonstrates	0 Does not demonstrate
1. The piece has been through multiple revisions and progress is evident.	5	4	3	2	1	0
2. A deep understanding of the work and its topic is communicated throughout the piece.	5	4	3	2	1	0
3. The work uses key elements to connect with the intended audience.	5	4	3	2	1	0
4. Purpose is reflected in the composition and arrangement of ideas.	5	4	3	2	1	0
5. The students takes calculated risks in working through the piece.	5	4	3	2	1	0
6. Sincere commitment to the work is evident.	5	4	3	2	1	0

www.educationcloset.com

Focused Authentic Integration Assessment Rubric

Student Name: _____ Task Focus: **Application**

Class: _____ Average Score: _____ / 30 = _____

Score Scale: 89-100% = 5   69-88% = 3   0-68% = 1

	5 Consistently demonstrates	4 Mostly demonstrates	3 Occasionally demonstrates	2 Demonstrates with assistance	1 Rarely demonstrates	0 Does not demonstrate
1. The piece naturally connects 2 or more ideas.	5	4	3	2	1	0
2. The work demonstrates the student's ability to transfer knowledge into practice.	5	4	3	2	1	0
3. The piece is original and demonstrates critical thinking.	5	4	3	2	1	0
4. The work clearly embeds aligned ideas throughout and uses skills/elements from a variety of areas.	5	4	3	2	1	0
5. The piece demonstrates a deep understanding of the topic.	5	4	3	2	1	0
6. The work is compelling and shares a unique perspective.	5	4	3	2	1	0

www.educationcloset.com

Focused Authentic Integration Assessment Rubric

Student Name: _____   Task Focus: **Presentation**

Class: _____   Average Score: _____ / 30 = _____

Score Scale: 89-100% = 5   69-88% = 3   0-68% = 1

	5 Consistently demonstrates	4 Mostly demonstrates	3 Occasionally demonstrates	2 Demonstrates with assistance	1 Rarely demonstrates	0 Does not demonstrate
1. The piece is constructed with attention to detail in a way that enhances its meaning.	5	4	3	2	1	0
2. The work is varied in length as well as structure.	5	4	3	2	1	0
3. There is intentional and explicit use of key elements which add variety and style.	5	4	3	2	1	0
4. The finished work shows creativity and original thought in both its organization and presentation style.	5	4	3	2	1	0
5. The student has made thoughtful decisions in choosing how to share their meaning through the finished work.	5	4	3	2	1	0
6. The work is refined and showcases each selected element effectively.	5	4	3	2	1	0

www.educationcloset.com

Authentic Integration Assessment Rubric - Student Edition

Purpose

The intention of the Student Edition of the Integration Assessment Rubric is to provide students with a way to frame their work to best meet rigorous expectations, to self-assess their work both in process and as a finished product, and as a tool to provide peers with valuable feedback.

Structure

The structure of the Student Edition rubric is exactly the same as the Teacher Edition. The only changes are the use of a more student-friendly vocabulary in the definition, the scoring expectations and the Enduring Understanding Question.

Ways to Engage Students in Owning Their Learning Using the Rubric

This tool contains two main ways in which students can develop ownership of their learning and develop deeper understanding of the processes in which they are engaged. First, you can provide students with the complete rubric itself. As stated in the teacher edition, you may choose to focus student attention on one or two components, or on the rubric in its entirety. That depends on the topic and the standards of measure. Students can then use this to guide them through their work - as a type of "check in" as they move throughout the project - and as a way to assess their own learning and growth.

The second way to use this tool is through the Integration Peer Review. Each component in the student edition contains a corresponding Integration Peer Review Sheet. Students may use this sheet to score each others' work after they have scored their own. Student scores may then consist of a combined score from both their own assessment and that of a classmate. You may use this in addition to your own score, as a way to formatively assess work, or as a weighted element within the total score of the work.

Each Peer Integration Review contains an area for students to provide an explanation for their score of the work, as well as two pieces of positive feedback and one piece of feedback for reflection and growth purposes.

Authentic Integration Assessment Rubric - Student Edition

Concepts

I shared my ideas clearly using what I know.

5: My piece is clear. My connections make sense.

3: The ideas in my piece are clear, but I didn't include many details.

1: I didn't really answer the question and my ideas don't show what I mean.

Enduring Understanding Question: Is my work clear and are my ideas original?

Skills

I made an effort to seek out and use knowledge to get better at a task.

5: I use key pieces of knowledge to show that I can complete a task.

3: My work is on topic, but I didn't put in as much effort as I could have. My piece shows that I am working on getting better at a task.

1: My work doesn't share my knowledge and isn't on topic. The piece shows that I cannot complete this task.

Enduring Understanding Question: Did I use important knowledge and elements well to share my message?

Structure

I organized my work in a logical way to show my ideas.

5: I organized important information or elements to connect my ideas.

3: My work has structure, but it's hard to see the connection between my ideas.

1: My work is disorganized and does not connect ideas to the topic.

Enduring Understanding Question: Does my work share my ideas in a clear, organized way?

Development

I showed my growth in this area over time.

5: I edited this work several times. This works shows my personal understanding of this topic in a clear way.

3: I edited this work once and it shares my basic understanding of this topic.

1: I did not edit this work and it does not show my understanding of this topic.

Enduring Understanding Question: Does my work show how my understanding of this topic changed over time?

Application

I used what I know about this topic to create something new.

5: My work shows that I can make connections with 2 or more ideas to create something original.

3: My work shows my basic understanding of the topic, but the connections to other ideas is not natural.

1: I did not make any connections to other ideas in my work and it does not show my understanding of the topic.

Enduring Understanding Question: Does this piece make natural connections across ideas to create a work with an original message?

Presentation

I presented my work in a creative way that shares my full learning experience.

5: I used appropriate elements to share my knowledge and ideas on the topic in a meaningful way.

3: Parts of my work use appropriate elements to communicate my message. Others are awkward or choppy.

1: My work does not share the meaning of the topic and does not use any appropriate elements for communication.

Enduring Understanding Question: Does my presentation showcase my message in a way that is interesting to my audience?

www.educationcloset.com

Integration Peer Review

Reviewer Name: _____   Title of Work:_____

Peer's Name: _____   Class: _____

Concepts

I shared my ideas clearly using what I know.

5: My piece is clear. My connections make sense.

3: The ideas in my piece are clear, but I didn't include many details.

1: I didn't really answer the question and my ideas don't show what I mean.

Enduring Understanding Question: Is my work clear and are my ideas original?

What number did your peer rate themselves? _____

What is your rating of this work?   + _____

What is the combined score? _____

Please explain your rating using details from the work:

Please write two rounds of applause for this work:

Please write one suggestion for more practice:

Integration Peer Review

Reviewer Name: _____ Title of Work:_____

Peer's Name: _____ Class: _____

Skills
I made an effort to seek out and use knowledge to get better at a task.
5: I use key pieces of knowledge to show that I can complete a task.
3: My work is on topic, but I didn't put in as much effort as I could have. My piece shows that I am working on getting better at a task.
1: My work doesn't share my knowledge and isn't on topic. The piece shows that I cannot complete this task.
Enduring Understanding Question: Did I use important knowledge and elements well to share my message?

What number did your peer rate themselves? _____

What is your rating of this work?   +   _____

What is the combined score? _____

Please explain your rating using details from the work:

Please write two rounds of applause for this work:

Please write one suggestion for more practice:

Integration Peer Review

Reviewer Name: _____ Title of Work:_____

Peer's Name: _____ Class: _____

Structure

I organized my work in a logical way to show my ideas.

5: I organized important information or elements to connect my ideas.

3: My work has structure, but it's hard to see the connection between my ideas.

1: My work is disorganized and does not connect ideas to the topic.

Enduring Understanding Question: Does my work share my ideas in a clear, organized way?

What number did your peer rate themselves? _____

What is your rating of this work? _____

$+$

What is the combined score? _____

Please explain your rating using details from the work:

Please write two rounds of applause for this work:

Please write one suggestion for more practice:

Integration Peer Review

Reviewer Name: _____   Title of Work:_____

Peer's Name: _____   Class: _____

Development

I showed my growth in this area over time.

5: I edited this work several times. This works shows my personal understanding of this topic in a clear way.

3: I edited this work once and it shares my basic understanding of this topic.

1: I did not edit this work and it does not show my understanding of this topic.

Enduring Understanding Question: Does my work show how my understanding of this topic changed over time?

What number did your peer rate themselves? _____

What is your rating of this work?   +   _____

What is the combined score? _____

Please explain your rating using details from the work:

Please write two rounds of applause for this work:

Please write one suggestion for more practice:

Integration Peer Review

Reviewer Name: _____   Title of Work: _____

Peer's Name: _____   Class: _____

Application

I used what I know about this topic to create something new.

5: My work shows that I can make connections with 2 or more ideas to create something original.

3: My work shows my basic understanding of the topic, but the connections to other ideas is not natural.

1: I did not make any connections to other ideas in my work and it does not show my understanding of the topic.

Enduring Understanding Question: Does this piece make natural connections across ideas to create a work with an original message?

What number did your peer rate themselves? _____

What is your rating of this work? $+$ _____

What is the combined score? _____

Please explain your rating using details from the work:

Please write two rounds of applause for this work:

Please write one suggestion for more practice:

Integration Peer Review

Reviewer Name: _____   Title of Work:_____

Peer's Name: _____   Class: _____

Presentation

I presented my work in a creative way that shares my full learning experience.

5: I used appropriate elements to share my knowledge and ideas on the topic in a meaningful way.

3: Parts of my work use appropriate elements to communicate my message. Others are awkward or choppy.

1: My work does not share the meaning of the topic and does not use any appropriate elements for communication.

Enduring Understanding Question: Does my presentation showcase my message in a way that is interesting to my audience?

What number did your peer rate themselves?   _____

What is your rating of this work?   +   _____

What is the combined score?   _____

Please explain your rating using details from the work:

Please write two rounds of applause for this work:

Please write one suggestion for more practice:

Data Daze

Assessments are changing to reflect a more robust, integrated approach to education that comes with the Common Core State Standards. It's important to recognize both the possibilities and the challenges that lie within this new era of assessment data. Data is king in the world of education, but all data changes depending on the lens through which you are viewing it. When using the assessment strategies in this section, it is important to know what data you are looking at, what it's limitations are in telling you about student achievement, and the very focused information it can target about a student's comprehension and growth. As you gather this data, be sure to synthesize it for yourself and others in a way that is valid and reliable. Use the metrics that are provided as a tool to make decisions about what instruction needs to occur next in order to move students' growth forward.

When looking at the data you collect, be sure to think about or ask the following questions when completing a data review:

1. What data was I trying to collect with this assessment? What do I want to know about my students' learning?
2. What does this data tell me?
3. What does this data NOT tell me?
4. What complexity factors (attendance, student groups, prior knowledge, parental support, scheduling, etc) may have affected this data?
5. As the teacher, what does this data reflect of my performance?
6. What professional development do I need to more effectively teach this material to these students?
7. What are the next steps in terms of instruction that we need to take to move students forward in their learning?

Let's look at why each of these questions are critical to the assessment conversation:

Question	Why it's Important
1. What data was I trying to collect with this assessment? What do I want to know about my students' learning?	You need to know what you're looking for to be able to analyze data appropriately. Your focus should be evident in your assessment selection and the data you gathered.
2. What does this data tell me?	Data is a measurement tool. It can be interpreted in many different ways, but when you first begin, you must look at the raw information and what it tells you before you begin making conclusions.
3. What does this data NOT tell me?	Just as it's important to see specific items that the data shares, it's also critical to know what that data cannot possibly tell you. It cannot tell you if a student was having a bad day, or if a student is "good or bad" at something. It can only share information at a set point in time. Be sure to recognize what the data cannot reflect so that you know its limitations.
4. What complexity factors (attendance, student groups, prior knowledge, parental support, scheduling, etc) may have affected this data?	Every classroom has a set of complexity factors beyond the teacher's control, and no two classrooms are alike. You must account for the fact that there are variances so that the data conversations can be authentic in their representation of student achievement.
5. As the teacher, what does this data reflect of my performance?	No teacher likes to hear this, but we all have things that we could do better in our classrooms. We also all have things that make us great teachers. When looking at the data, a teacher must do a certain amount of self-reflection on what they contributed to those results and the steps they can take to continue to improve as a practitioner. This is just part of good teaching.

Question	Why it's Important
6. What professional development do I need to more effectively teach this material to these students?	None of us can know everything. Professional development is a key component in continuing the learning journey and is an appropriate step in providing the best strategies and ideas for our students in the classroom.
7. What are the next steps in terms of instruction that we need to take to move students forward in their learning?	This is a key step, but it cannot come before the other steps have been completed. Once you have a full, clear picture of the data from your assessment, you need to determine what comes next in terms of teaching and learning for your students to make them as successful as possible.

Here is a blank data form that you can use to help you with these conversations:

Question	Insights
1. What data was I trying to collect with this assessment? What do I want to know about my students' learning?	
2. What does this data tell me?	
3. What does this data NOT tell me?	
4. What complexity factors (attendance, student groups, prior knowledge, parental support, scheduling, etc) may have affected this data?	
5. As the teacher, what does this data reflect of my performance?	
6. What professional development do I need to more effectively teach this material to these students?	
7. What are the next steps in terms of instruction that we need to take to move students forward in their learning?	

It's important to have these rich dialogues about what the assessments tell us about student learning and our own teaching because it's the only way we will continue to make progress. Assessment tools, whether they be summative, formative, portfolio or performance, are merely the diagnostics that we use to inform us of what is happening with our students and how we can best assist them to meeting their full potential. Assessments themselves are useless if we cannot use them to improve student achievement, and this is not possible without the critical data conversations.

An Assessment Wrap-Up

Obviously, there are many ways to assess all contents, as well as integrated lessons. You will need to choose the right way for your students at the right time in your classroom. The suggestions given in this book are only given with the knowledge that teachers everywhere are struggling with ways to authentically measure student achievement in ways that represent the whole package of student learning. As we continue to develop and implement researched best practices in differentiated instruction, integrated learning and embedding technology within the classroom as a pathway for student learning and representation, assessments need to change to reflect those new outcomes. The craft of teaching becomes the informed decisions that teachers make as to what form of assessment most directly portrays student learning and growth with integrity.

The assessments on these pages, particularly the performance assessments, have been informed by a variety of sources in order to provide an assessment that can be used with consistency and which addresses the unique complexities of an integrated lesson. As discussed in the beginning of this section, summative assessments have traditionally been the place that we turn when looking for consistent, standardized assessment of information on a subject. These assessment strategies in this section seek to provide an alternative which embeds rigorous, high-quality standards of assessment with the key elements and components of a wide range of subject areas. As you consider their use in your classroom, remember that these are a guide and you can always edit them to meet the needs of your class or lesson. When working with integration, flexibility within a framework is they key.

A word of caution: use these suggested assessment strategies with care and consideration. Do not assume that any assessment will work for every situation. Many fine arts and STEM teachers are weary of the assessments provided on this page, not because of their quality, but because of how they will be used to interpret their content areas. As with all integrated lessons, it's critical to select, implement and review the data from these assessments in close relationship to the content area with which you are integrating. This ensures that the assessments being given are representative of the areas for which you are seeking to measure student understanding and application.

As we close this book, please know that teaching in an integrated way, whether it be through STEM, Arts Integration, or any other version, is a meaningful and exciting journey. It truly is about the process and not the product - for both you and your students. But it is difficult and challenging to implement successfully without the appropriate tools along the way. When you are getting lost in the process, come back to this book for tools, suggestions, inspiration and guidance to help you on your path to sharing a world-class education with your students. It can only go up from here!

Appendix A: The Elements

The Elements of *Dance*

*M*ovement

*__Locomotor__: Movement through space from one point to another (walk, run, jump, hop, leap, skip, gallop, slide, roll)
*__Non-Locomotor:__ Movement around the body's axis (bend, twist, stretch, push, pull, swing, shake, circle, sway, carve, fall, melt, turn, kick, press, rise, sink, burst, wiggle)

*B*ody

*__Shape:__ A frozen pose (curves, straight, angular, twisted, narrow, wide, symmetrical, asymmetrical)
*__Part:__ Body parts (head, eyes, torso, shoulder, arms, fingers, elbows, hands, hips, legs, knees, feet, ankles, etc)

*S*pace

* __Shelf Space:__ Space immediately around the body
*__General Space:__ Space throughout the room
*__Level:__ High, medium or low
*__Direction:__ Forward, backward, sideways, up, down
*__Pathway:__ Curved, straight, zigzag, diagonal
*__Size:__ Big, small, narrow, wide
*__Focus:__ Direction of gaze

*T*ime

*__Tempo__: Fast, medium, slow
*__Rhythm:__ A succession of movement or sounds of various duration.

*E*nergy

*__Weight:__ Strong (heavy, firm, powerful), light (gentle, soft)
*__Flow:__ Free (continuous, fluid movement), bound (restrained, controlled)
*__Quality:__ Sharp, sudden, smooth, sustained, tight, loose, suspended, collapsed, heavy, weak, percussive

The Elements of Design

Balance
Arrange art elements to create a feeling of stability. *symmetrical, format, asymmetrical, informal, radial

Movement
Combining art elements to produce a look or feel of action.

Repetition
Combining art elements so that the same element(s) are used over and over again.

Gradation
Combining art elements by using a series of gradual changes in those elements, usually a step-by-step change. Layering.

Proprotion
Relationship of various elements of art to the whole composition and to each other. Size relationships

Empasis/Contrast
Combining elements to stress the differences between those elements and to create one or more centers of interest.

Variety
Combining art elements in involved ways to achieve intricate and complex relationships.

Adapted from M. Barbosa MATI 2010 definitions; Based on definitions from the MD Department of Education Visual Arts Glossary

The Elements of *Drama*

Space
✓ Where you **perform** (stage, chair, immediate surrounding area)
✓ Where **action** occurs (the distance between characters, settings)

Time
✓ When in **history**
✓ Period of the **day**

Imitation
Reproduction of **thoughts** and **ideas**.

Action
✓ Movement of **people**.
✓ Movement of the **story**.

Language
Communicating through
✓ **Written** Word
✓ **Verbal** Word

Energy
The **intensity** with which you **engage** with the piece.

The Elements of Music

Pitch
Moving from one distance of sound to another. **High to low.**

Duration
The amount of time a sound occurs.
- ✓ **Long** (whole notes, half notes) or
- ✓ **Short** (quarter notes, eighth notes, sixteenth notes).

Dynamics
The sound level at which music is played.
- ✓ **Loud** (forte, fortissimo) or
- ✓ **Soft** (piano, pianissimo).
- ✓ **Medium** is often called **mezzo-piano** (pronounced "met-so pi-ah-no") or **mezzo-forte** (pronounced "met-so four-tay").

Tone Color
The quality of sound, what the voice or instrument sounds like. This is also referred to as "**Timbre**" (pronounced tam-ber).
* <u>Examples include</u>: **light, airy, dark, mystical, rich, full, dancing, excited.**

Form
The organization of music.
Examples include:
- ✓ **ABA** (first section, second section, first section repeats)
- ✓ **AB** (first section, followed by second section)
- ✓ **Rondo** (ABACA - The A section always comes after each new section).

Texture
The layers of sound within a piece of music. Examples include:
- ✓ Just **melody** (monophony) or
- ✓ **Melody and harmony** (polyphony).
- ✓ **Chords** (3 or more notes played at the same time).
- ✓ Instruments can add to the texture of music: blaring, rough, smooth, choppy, disjointed, tight, rich.

The Elements of *Visual Art*

Line
A continuous mark on a surface by a moving point. **<u>Open</u>** from the beginning to the ending.
* Outline, contour, silhouette.

Shape
A visual element that has two dimensions: length and width. **<u>Closed.</u>**
*Square, triangle, circle, free-form, geometric, organic

Color
Properties of **<u>hue</u>** (red, blue, etc.), **<u>intensity</u>** (purity and strength of a color), and **<u>value</u>** (lightness or darkness).

Form
<u>Three-dimensional</u> (having height, width and depth) and which **<u>encloses volume</u>**.
* cubes, spheres, pyramids, and cylinders.

Texture
Surface Qualities. The **<u>look or feel</u>** of objects.
* rough, smooth, glassy, blurry, silky, wooly.

Value
Describes the **lightness or darkness** of a color. Gradual changes in drawings, woodcuts, photographs, etc. even when color is absent.

Space
<u>Two or three-dimensional</u> in reference to the distance or area **<u>between, around, above, below or within</u>** objects.

Appendix B: Additional Materials

Lesson: Reading the Art

Link: Robinson Crusoe Illustration No. 13, NC Wyeth: http://www.artpassions.net/galleries/wyeth/crusoe13.jpg

Routine: Think, Puzzle, Explore

Source: http://pzweb.harvard.edu/vt/visiblethinking_html_files/03_thinkingroutines/03d_understandingroutines/ThinkPuzzleExplore/ThinkPuzzleExplore_Routine.html

Think

Puzzle

Explore

What do you think you know about a topic?

What questions do you have?

What does this topic make you want to explore?

Lesson: Shape Shifter

I See....

What do you see in
the selected piece?

I Think....

What do you think
about this work?

I Wonder....

What do you wonder
about this work?

Lesson: Stippling Graphs

Stippling Technique

Stippling is an artistic process all based on the use of dots. You can use thick dots, thin dots, a variety of colors, space them out, bunch them together - whatever your heart desires in making your vision become a reality.

Steps:

1. View several examples of artwork using the Stippling process and have students reflect on what they see.

2. Give each student a clean piece of white paper and a variety of markers in color and tip.

3. Use the tip of the marker to make a pattern of dots.

4. Create the effect of shading by filling in areas with close stippled dots.

5. Combine dots of various colors to mix colors visually.

Example:

Lesson: Founders' Drama

John Adams' Speech to the Second Continental Congress

Source: http://bit.ly/WyEcvF

Given Monday, July 1, 1776, Adams. "Adams was the Atlas of the hour, the man to whom the country is more indebted for the great measure of independency...He it was who sustained the debate, and by the force of his reasoning demonstrated not only the justice, but the expediency of the measure." - New Jersey delegate Richard Stockton

The vote for independence took place the next day, on July 2, 1776.

Text of Speech, pieced together from letters and Adams' recollections as an old man:

"*Measures of the most stupendous magnitude - measures which affect the lives of millions, born and unborn - are now before us. We must expect a great expense of blood and pain, but we must remember that a free constitution of civil government cannot be purchased at too dear a rate, as there is nothing this side of Jerusalem of greater importance to mankind. My worthy colleague from Pennsylvania has spoken with grace and eloquence, and he has given you a grim prognostication of our nation future, but where he foresees apocalypse, I see hope. I see a new nation ready to take its place in the world. Not an empire, but a Republic, and a republic of laws, not men.*

Gentlemen, we are in the very midst of revolution, the most complete, unexpected and remarkable of any in the history of the world. How few of the human race have ever had an opportunity of choosing a system of government for themselves and their children.

I am not without apprehensions, gentlemen. But the end we have in sight is more than worth all the means. I believe, Sirs, that the hour has come. My judgment approves this measure, and my whole heart is in it. All that I have, all that I am, and all that I hope in this life I am now ready to stake upon it.

While I live, let me have a country. A free country."

Appendix C: National Arts Standards and Maryland STEM Standards of Practice

VISUAL ARTS

Source: http://www.arteducators.org/store/NAEA_Natl_Visual_Standards1.pdf

1. Understanding and applying media, techniques, and processes.
2. Using knowledge of structures and functions.
3. Choosing and evaluating a range of subject matter, symbols, and ideas.
4. Understanding the visual arts in relation to history and cultures.
5. Reflecting upon and assessing the characteristics and merits of their work and the work of others.
6. Making connections between visual arts and other disciplines.

MUSIC

Source: http://musiced.nafme.org/resources/national-standards-for-music-education/

1. Singing, alone and with others, a varied repertoire of music.
2. Performing on instruments, alone and with others, a varied repertoire of music.
3. Improvising melodies, variations, and accompaniments.
4. Composing and arranging music within specified guidelines.
5. Reading and notating music.
6. Listening to, analyzing, and describing music.
7. Evaluating music and music performances.
8. Understanding relationships between music, the other arts, and disciplines outside the arts.
9. Understanding music in relation to history and culture.

DANCE

Source: http://www.aahperd.org/nda/profDevelopment/standards9-12.cfm

1. Identifying and demonstrating movement elements and skills in performing dance.
2. Understanding the choreographic principles, processes, and structures.
3. Understanding dance as a way to create and communicate meaning.
4. Applying and demonstrating critical and creative thinking skills in dance.

5. Demonstrating and understanding dance in various cultures and historical periods.

6. Making connections between dance and healthful living.

7. Making connections between dance and other disciplines.

THEATRE

Source: http://www.aate.com/?page=NationalStandards

1. Script writing by planning and recording improvisations based on personal experience and heritage, imagination, literature, and history.

2. Acting by assuming roles and interacting in improvisations.

3. Designing by visualizing and arranging environments for classroom dramatizations.

4. Directing by planning classroom dramatizations.

5. Researching by finding information to support classroom dramatizations.

6. Comparing and connecting art forms by describing theatre, dramatic media (such as film, television, and electronic media), and other art forms.

7. Analyzing and explaining personal preferences and constructing meanings from classroom dramatizations and from theatre, film, television, and electronic media productions.

8. Understanding context by recognizing the role of theatre, film, television, and electronic media in daily life.

Maryland STEM Standards of Practice

Source: http://www.marylandpublicschools.org/MSDE/programs/stem/

1. Learn and Apply Rigorous Science, Technology, Engineering, and Mathematics Content.

2. Integrate Science, Technology, Engineering, and Mathematics Content.

3. Interpret and Communicate STEM Information.

4. Engage in Inquiry.

5. Engage in Logical Reasoning.

6. Collaborate as a STEM Team.

7. Apply Technology Appropriately.

Artistic Habits of Mind

Source: http://www.pz.harvard.edu/research/StudioThink/StudioThinkEight.htm

1. **Develop Craft:** Learning to use and care for tools. Learning artistic conventions.

2. **Engage and Persist:** Learning to embrace problems of relevance within the art world and/or of personal importance, to develop focus and other mental states conducive to working and persevering at art tasks.

3. **Envision:** Learning to picture mentally what cannot be directly observed and imagine possible next steps in making a piece.

4. **Express:** Learning to create works that convey an idea, a feeling or a personal meaning.

5. **Observe:** Learning to attend to visual contexts more closely than ordinary "looking" requires, and thereby to see things that otherwise might not be seen.

6. **Reflect:** Learning to think and talk with others about an aspect of one's work or process.

7. **Stretch and Explore:** Learning to reach beyond one's capacities, to explore playfully without a preconceived plan, and to embrace the opportunity to learn from mistakes and accidents.

8. **Understand Art World:** Learning to interact as an artist with other artists and within the broader society.

Appendix D: Common Core Anchor Standards

College and Career Readiness Anchor Standards: Reading

Source: http://www.corestandards.org/ELA-Literacy/CCRA/R

Key Ideas and Details

- CCSS.ELA-Literacy.CCRA.R.1 Read closely to determine what the text says explicitly and to make logical inferences from it; cite specific textual evidence when writing or speaking to support conclusions drawn from the text.

- CCSS.ELA-Literacy.CCRA.R.2 Determine central ideas or themes of a text and analyze their development; summarize the key supporting details and ideas.

- CCSS.ELA-Literacy.CCRA.R.3 Analyze how and why individuals, events, or ideas develop and interact over the course of a text.

Craft and Structure

- CCSS.ELA-Literacy.CCRA.R.4 Interpret words and phrases as they are used in a text, including determining technical, connotative, and figurative meanings, and analyze how specific word choices shape meaning or tone.

- CCSS.ELA-Literacy.CCRA.R.5 Analyze the structure of texts, including how specific sentences, paragraphs, and larger portions of the text (e.g., a section, chapter, scene, or stanza) relate to each other and the whole.

- CCSS.ELA-Literacy.CCRA.R.6 Assess how point of view or purpose shapes the content and style of a text.

Integration of Knowledge and Ideas

- CCSS.ELA-Literacy.CCRA.R.7 Integrate and evaluate content presented in diverse media and formats, including visually and quantitatively, as well as in words.[1]

- CCSS.ELA-Literacy.CCRA.R.8 Delineate and evaluate the argument and specific claims in a text, including the validity of the reasoning as well as the relevance and sufficiency of the evidence.

- CCSS.ELA-Literacy.CCRA.R.9 Analyze how two or more texts address similar themes or topics in order to build knowledge or to compare the approaches the authors take.

Range of Reading and Level of Text Complexity

- CCSS.ELA-Literacy.CCRA.R.10 Read and comprehend complex literary and informational texts independently and proficiently.

College and Career Readiness Anchor Standards: Writing

Source: http://www.corestandards.org/ELA-Literacy/CCRA/W

Text Types and Purposes

- CCSS.ELA-Literacy.CCRA.W.1 Write arguments to support claims in an analysis of substantive topics or texts using valid reasoning and relevant and sufficient evidence.

- CCSS.ELA-Literacy.CCRA.W.2 Write informative/explanatory texts to examine and convey complex ideas and information clearly and accurately through the effective selection, organization, and analysis of content.

- CCSS.ELA-Literacy.CCRA.W.3 Write narratives to develop real or imagined experiences or events using effective technique, well-chosen details and well-structured event sequences.

Production and Distribution of Writing

- CCSS.ELA-Literacy.CCRA.W.4 Produce clear and coherent writing in which the development, organization, and style are appropriate to task, purpose, and audience.

- CCSS.ELA-Literacy.CCRA.W.5 Develop and strengthen writing as needed by planning, revising, editing, rewriting, or trying a new approach.

- CCSS.ELA-Literacy.CCRA.W.6 Use technology, including the Internet, to produce and publish writing and to interact and collaborate with others.

Research to Build and Present Knowledge

- CCSS.ELA-Literacy.CCRA.W.7 Conduct short as well as more sustained research projects based on focused questions, demonstrating understanding of the subject under investigation.

- CCSS.ELA-Literacy.CCRA.W.8 Gather relevant information from multiple print and digital sources, assess the credibility and accuracy of each source, and integrate the information while avoiding plagiarism.

- CCSS.ELA-Literacy.CCRA.W.9 Draw evidence from literary or informational texts to support analysis, reflection, and research.

Range of Writing

- CCSS.ELA-Literacy.CCRA.W.10 Write routinely over extended time frames (time for research, reflection, and revision) and shorter time frames (a single sitting or a day or two) for a range of tasks, purposes, and audiences.

College and Career Readiness Anchor Standards: Speaking and Listening

Source: http://www.corestandards.org/ELA-Literacy/CCRA/SL

Comprehension and Collaboration

- CCSS.ELA-Literacy.CCRA.SL.1 Prepare for and participate effectively in a range of conversations and collaborations with diverse partners, building on others' ideas and expressing their own clearly and persuasively.

- CCSS.ELA-Literacy.CCRA.SL.2 Integrate and evaluate information presented in diverse media and formats, including visually, quantitatively, and orally.

- CCSS.ELA-Literacy.CCRA.SL.3 Evaluate a speaker's point of view, reasoning, and use of evidence and rhetoric.

Presentation of Knowledge and Ideas

- CCSS.ELA-Literacy.CCRA.SL.4 Present information, findings, and supporting evidence such that listeners can follow the line of reasoning and the organization, development, and style are appropriate to task, purpose, and audience.

- CCSS.ELA-Literacy.CCRA.SL.5 Make strategic use of digital media and visual displays of data to express information and enhance understanding of presentations.

- CCSS.ELA-Literacy.CCRA.SL.6 Adapt speech to a variety of contexts and communicative tasks, demonstrating command of formal English when indicated or appropriate.

College and Career Readiness Anchor Standards: Language

Source: http://www.corestandards.org/ELA-Literacy/CCRA/L

Conventions of Standard English

- CCSS.ELA-Literacy.CCRA.L.1 Demonstrate command of the conventions of standard English grammar and usage when writing or speaking.

- CCSS.ELA-Literacy.CCRA.L.2 Demonstrate command of the conventions of standard English capitalization, punctuation, and spelling when writing.

Knowledge of Language

- CCSS.ELA-Literacy.CCRA.L.3 Apply knowledge of language to understand how language functions in different contexts, to make effective choices for meaning or style, and to comprehend more fully when reading or listening.

Vocabulary Acquisition and Use

- CCSS.ELA-Literacy.CCRA.L.4 Determine or clarify the meaning of unknown and multiple-meaning words and phrases by using context clues, analyzing meaningful word parts, and consulting general and specialized reference materials, as appropriate.

- CCSS.ELA-Literacy.CCRA.L.5 Demonstrate understanding of figurative language, word relationships, and nuances in word meanings.

- CCSS.ELA-Literacy.CCRA.L.6 Acquire and use accurately a range of general academic and domain-specific words and phrases sufficient for reading, writing, speaking, and listening at the college and career readiness level; demonstrate independence in gathering vocabulary knowledge when encountering an unknown term important to comprehension or expression.

Common Core Math: Standards of Mathematical Practice

Source: http://www.corestandards.org/assets/CCSSI_Math%20Standards.pdf

These are not the standards for mathematical content, but are rather the standards of mathematical practice which are taught K-12 and through which the standards for mathematical content are built.

1. Make sense of problems and persevere in solving them.

2. Reason abstractly and quantitatively.

3. Construct viable arguments and critique the reasoning of others.

4. Model with mathematics.

5. Use appropriate tools strategically.

6. Attend to precision.

7. Look for and make use of structure.

8. Look for and express regularity in repeated reasoning.

additional
REFERENCES & RESOURCES

Aprill, A., Burnaford, G., Weiss, C. (2001). *Renaissance in the Classroom: Arts Integration and Meaningful Learning.* New York, New York: Routledge.

Blair, K., Ganley, P, and Glass, D. (2012). *Universal Design for Learning in the Classroom Practical Applications.* New York, New York: Guilford Press.

Cremin, T., Goouch, K., Blakemore, L., Goff, E., & Macdonald, R. (2006). *Connecting drama and writing: Seizing the moment to write. Research in Drama Education: The Journal of Applied Theatre and Performance, 11(3), 273 - 291.*

Culham, R. (2003). *6 + 1 Traits of Writing: The Complete Guide, Grades 3 and Up.* New York, New York: Scholastic Professional Books.

DeMoss, K. & Morris, T. (2002). *How arts integration supports student learning: Students shed light on the connections. Chicago, IL: Chicago Arts Partnerships in Education (CAPE).*

Donahue, D. and Stuart, J. (2010). *Artful Teaching: Integrating the Arts for Understanding Across the Curriculum, K-8.* New York, New York: Teachers College Press.

Fogarty, R. (October, 1991). Ten Ways to Integrate Curriculum. *Educational Leadership*, pg. 61-65.

Jacobs, H. (1997). *Mapping the Big Picture: Integrating Curriculum and Assessment, K-12.* Alexandria, Virginia: Association for Supervision & Curriculum Development.

McTighe, J. and Wiggins, G. (2005). *Understanding by Design, Expanded 2nd Edition.* Alexandria, Virginia: Association for Supervision & Curriculum Development.

Moga, E., Burger, K., Hetland, L., & Winner, E. (2000). Does studying the arts engender creative thinking? Evidence for near but not far transfer. *Journal of Aesthetic Education, 34 (3/4), 91-104.*

November, A. (2012). *Who Owns the Learning?: Preparing Students for Success in the Digital Age.* Bloomington, Indiana: Solution Tree.

Riley, S. (2012). *Shake the Sketch: An Arts Integration Workbook.* Charleston, South Carolina: CreateSpace.

Tishman, S., MacGillivray, D., & Palmer, P. (1999). *Investigating the educational impact and potential of the Museum of Modern Art's Visual Thinking Curriculum: Final report.* Cambridge, MA: Harvard Project Zero.

Partnership for Assessment of Readiness for College and Careers Website: http://www.parcconline.org/parcc-assessment-design

Project Zero (Harvard University) Research Website: http://www.pz.harvard.edu/Research/Research.htm

Universal Design for Learning Website, http://www.cast.org/udl/index.html

ACKNOWLEDGEMENTS

This book would not have been possible without a tremendous number of people, talents, research, and reviews. I sincerely appreciate everyone who has been generous of their time, skills, expertise and mentoring abilities to help guide and shape my work. Please take a moment to read their names and know that these are some of the most brilliant people that I have had the pleasure to work with and know.

Many thanks go to my mentors in Arts Integration and my professional learning community members who push me to learn and grow everyday. Among them are Elizabeth Peterson, Jessica Balsley, Melissa Edwards, Shelly Terrell, Angela Maiers, and Scott McLeod. I read everything you write and take in all of your brilliant ideas. You make me a better educator and person and for that I am grateful.

To the people that I work with daily at Anne Arundel County Public Schools, I am in awe of your talent and your tenacity. You truly are some of the brightest and best in education and you are too often not given the credit you are due. This one is for you.

To Amy Cohn - no awards could ever measure the success and impact that you have everyday on teachers and children. Thank you for always cheering me on and pushing me to strive for perfection.

To Sue Owens and Eleni Dykstra - You. are. fabulous.

To Greg Pilewski and Andrea Kane - You are both by far some of the best visionaries I have ever met for district-level leadership. I learn so much simply by watching you each and every day and I consider myself fortunate to be a part of your tremendous mission. Thank you for each and every opportunity to have placed before me, and for being great friends along the way.

To my family, John, Ginger, Andrew, Diana, Warren, Art, Vickie, Kim, Dave, Connor, Peyton and Aileen - words cannot express the overwhelming blessings you each bring to my life. Thank you for being patient with me, for accepting my faults and for celebrating my successes and for being my firm foundation.

To my husband Kevin and my daughter, Emma Kate - you are the loves of my life. You teach me about the amazing capacity of love and I am so incredibly humbled by our life together. Thank you for walking beside me each and every day. I love you.

a b o u t
THE AUTHOR

Susan Riley is an arts integration specialist, based out of Maryland. She earned her Bachelor of Music degree from Westminster Choir College in Princeton, NJ and her Masters of Science degree in Education Administration and Supervision from McDaniel College in Westminster, MD. Susan focuses on teacher professional development in arts integration, Common Core State Standards, 21st century learning skills, and technology. Susan is the founder and curator of EducationCloset.com, a website dedicated to Arts Integration and Innovation. Here, she and her team write about teaching and leadership ideas, as well as providing free Arts Integration lesson plans, a vibrant online community and a wealth of resources for educators looking to connect with the Common Core State Standards.

Additionally, Susan also has written articles for several online magazines, guest authored posts on various professional blogs including Americans for the Arts and Edutopia and has authored two other books: Shake the Sketch: An Arts Integration Workbook and A Vocal Advocate.

Susan lives in Westminster, Maryland with her husband Kevin and daughter Emma Kate.

You can contact Susan directly at: susan@educationcloset.com

OCT 0 5 2016